The Claude Neal Lynching

*The 1934 Murders of
Claude Neal and Lola Cannady*

Dale Cox

2012

Visit the author online at:

www.exploresouthernhistory.com

Old Kitchen Books
4523 Oak Grove Road
Bascom, Florida 32423

*"But let justice roll down like waters,
and righteousness like an ever-flowing stream."*
Amos 5:24.

"Hatred stirs up strife, but love covers all offenses."
Proverbs 10:12

This book is respectfully dedicated to the memory of Deputy Dave Ham. He gave his life in the service of his neighbors, family and friends.

Table of Contents

Maps

Introduction

On October 18, 1934, a young woman named Lola Cannady was raped and murdered in a rural farm community in Jackson County, Florida. Eight days later her accused killer, a farm laborer named Claude Neal, was tortured and killed by a group of six men deep in the woods of eastern Jackson County.

The two murders were horribly violent. Claude Neal and Lola Cannady were both deprived of their civil rights, their lives and ultimately justice in the courts. Both are buried in unmarked graves. And yet for reasons that modern writers and historians seem unable to explain, only one of them has been the focus of any modern outrage and concern. Thousands of pages have been written about the killing of Claude Neal, very few about the murder of Lola Cannady.

As this book was being prepared for press simple internet searches demonstrated the disparity in the way modern academics, journalists and commentators view the two victims. The search terms "Claude Neal" and "lynching" produced 114,000 results. The search terms "Lola Cannady" and "murder" returned only 212.

Even more shocking is the fact that while more than 3,500 books and journals have discussed the events of 1934, not a single one has used the correct spelling of Lola Cannady's name. In the rare instances that her name is given at all, it is usually misspelled as "Lola Cannidy." In more than 3,000 publications she is identified only as a "white girl" or "white woman."

It is troubling that so many writers and historians, some of them highly regarded in their fields, could care so little about the victim of a horrible murder that they would not take time even to verify the spelling of her name. Equally troubling is the tidal wave of incorrect information and outright falsehood that has obscured the truth of what happened in Jackson County in 1934. Evidence has been misrepresented or completely ignored, rumors and innuendo have been treated as fact, utter falsehoods have been written about law enforcement officers. Even the common description of Neal's death as the "last public spectacle" lynching is false. He was not lynched in public and, sadly, public spectacle lynching did not end with his death.

Two people were brutally murdered in the rural fields and woods of Jackson County in October of 1934. Neither received legal justice and neither is more or less deserving of remembrance than the other. And yet the simple truth is that one has been remembered by America's academics and the other has not.

When I began writing this book, I did so because I considered the events surrounding the 1934 murders of Claude Neal and Lola Cannady to be of historical significance. I did not know nor did I expect that events from seventy-seven years ago would be thrust back into the headlines with the news that the U.S. Department of Justice was conducting a new investigation into the case (or at least into the part of it dealing with Claude Neal). And yet that is exactly what happened. In the fall of 2011, newspapers across the country reported that agents from the Federal Bureau of Investigation were again looking into the circumstances of the Claude Neal lynching.

The *St. Petersburg Times*, *Tallahassee Democrat* and other major Florida newspapers ran new stories and columns on the lynching. Jackson County and the events that happened there in 1934 became common fodder for internet discussion and debate. The debate intensified when a man identifying himself as a nephew of Claude Neal demanded $77 million in reparations from the federal, state and local governments.

The Neal lynching, it seemed, was no longer the fare of historians, but of modern investigators and journalists. There is something surreal about this. All of the men responsible for the murder are dead, some of them for many, many years. Jackson County of 2011 is not the Jackson County of 1934 and, in truth, the county seventy-seven years ago was far different than it has generally been described by most writers dealing with the lynching and related events.

It is worth noting that of the various newspapers and websites that ran reports on the reopening of the lynching investigation, I have not been able to find a single one that also ran stories on unsolved lynching deaths in their own communities. And yet in each of the cities that I checked, there are most definitely unsolved lynching cases. Some of them, in fact, involved more deaths and were much more public spectacles than the Jackson County killing. Perhaps it is easier to see ugliness in people and places far removed from you than in your own community? A rural place like Jackson County, with a population of under 50,000, is a much easier community to target than, say, counties like Leon (Tallahassee) and Pinellas (St. Petersburg), which have populations of more than 275,000 and 916,000 respectively.

The more I followed the publicity surrounding the renewed investigation of the Neal lynching, the more determined I became that this book would be written with no agenda other than to tell the real truth about what happened in Jackson County in 1934, to both Claude Neal and Lola Cannady. This determination quickly proved controversial. Before a single person had read even one line of the book, the very fact that I was working on it and had been quoted as saying that it would offer a detailed history of both murders ignited a firestorm of debate and criticism. Emails poured in, accusing me of being naïve at best and racist at worst. More than a few of the people posting comments on a Tampa Bay area news website urged that I be prosecuted as an accessory to murder, even though I was born nearly thirty years after Claude Neal and Lola Cannady were killed. This is the eleventh work of history I've written and I've never been vilified before or, to the best of my knowledge, even after one came out in print. It was definitely a new experience.

This book will present a large amount of previously unpublished material and evidence regarding the murders of Lola Cannady and Claude Neal. It is a work of chronological history, not a study in sociology, ethics or psychology. The goal is to present an accurate and balanced history of two violent weeks that took place nearly eighty years ago. I hope the narrative that follows will provide some clarity to the events that took place in Jackson County in October of 1934, while also presenting an accurate review of the evidence, investigations and aftermath of the murders.

A number of people contributed significantly to the completion of this book. Special recognition is due to four individuals that have passed from among us. E.W. Carswell was a noted historian and friend; Sarah Bruce Harris was the first archivist of Jackson County and one of my mentors; John Winslett was an employee of the Jackson County Floridan in 1934, and Roy Beall, Sr., was a businessman, civic leader and honorable gentleman. All assisted materially in uncovering original documentation and locating surviving eyewitnesses when I first began researching the Cannady and Neal murders more than thirty years ago. I miss them all.

My son, William C. Cox, offered invaluable assistance in the writing of this book. Not only did he read chapters as they were finished and offer suggestions, he assisted with research and accompanied me on visits to sites associated with the murders. I could not have finished this book without his help and I am very proud and grateful that I had the chance to work on it with him.

My youngest son, Alan P. Cox, also assisted by discussing the crimes, visiting related sites and offering input. I am likewise grateful and proud that I was able to work with him.

My mother, Pearl L. Cox, took time to read the manuscript and offer suggestions. I greatly appreciate her assistance.

Sheriff John P. McDaniel (retired) is a lawman who knows better than most the true cost and horror of crime. He was sheriff of Jackson County for three decades, an office that he held with integrity. It was my honor to spend considerable time with him unraveling many of the details of the murder of Lola Cannady and lynching of Claude Neal when he looked into the cases while compiling historical information on his department in 1986-1988.

Noted genealogist Cindy Sloan assisted in locating census data, historical newspaper articles, death certificates and other source material. Archival expert Sue Tindel of the office of Jackson County Clerk of Courts Dale Guthrie helped in locating original grand jury, land and other records. Historian Daniel T. Weinfeld assisted in locating original NAACP records, a copy of the Pathe newsreel footage of the post-lynching Marianna riot and other material. I am very grateful to all three and would not have been able to complete this project without their assistance.

My sincere appreciation is also due to the staffs of the following libraries and archives for allowing access to their holdings: the National Archives, Library of Congress, Florida State Archives, Florida State Library, Alabama State Archives, Special Collections Department of the John C. Pace Library at the University of West Florida, Special Collections Department of the Strozier Library at Florida State University, the P.K. Yonge Library of Florida History at the University of Florida, the W.C. Bradley Library in Columbus, Georgia, the Dougherty County Public Library in Albany, Georgia, the Columbia Public Library in Columbia, South Carolina, the Willard Library in Evansville, Indiana, and the Bay County Public Library in Panama City, Florida.

Many others, too numerous to name, provided information that assisted in the writing of this book. My sincere gratitude is extended to them all.

Dale Cox

2011

The Claude Neal Lynching

The 1934 Murders of
Claude Neal and Lola Cannady

Dale Cox

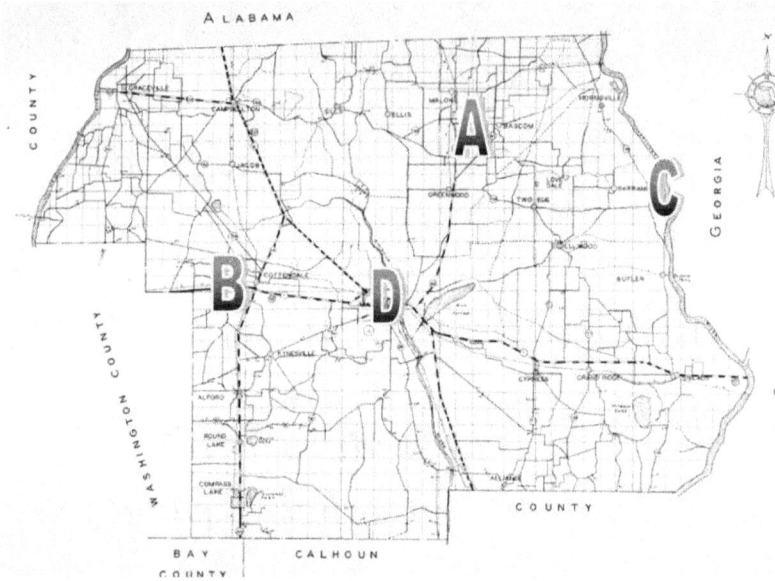

Jackson County, Florida
October 1934

A. Cannady Farm

B. Escape Attempt Site

C. Peri Landing (Lynching Site)

D. Marianna

Scale: Each Mark = 1 Mile

CHAPTER ONE

Shadows of the Past

In the summer and fall of 2011, the United States Department of Justice opened a civil rights investigation into the 1934 lynching of Claude Neal. It was, so far as is known, the first time that agents from the Federal Bureau of Investigation looked into the crime and was part of a wider investigation of as many as 100 historical crimes opened during the administration of President George W. Bush.. While funding for such efforts was reduced under President Barack Obama, the investigations have continued.

"(H)ate-crimes enforcement, and cold-case investigations in particular, remain a priority to this administration," Justice Department Spokesperson Xochitl Hinojosa told reporters in July of 2011, "and the Civil Rights Division will devote the resources necessary to fully investigate all significant matters." While the department would not confirm details, one of those specific matters was the Claude Neal lynching. FBI agents were in Jackson County interviewing current and former public officials and conducting records research at the Jackson County Courthouse in Marianna. Seventy-seven years had passed since the horrible events of 1934.[1]

It was not, of course, the first time that the shadows of that fateful year had lingered over Jackson County, nor will it be the last. The story of the Claude Neal lynching, however, is not just a story of extralegal justice in the years of the Great Depression, it is a story of violence and murder. It began when the life of a young woman named Lola Cannady was taken in the farm country near Greenwood, Florida, on a clear and cool October afternoon.

Lola Cannady was, by all accounts, a bright and cheerful young woman. Friendly with a kind word for all she met, she was small in stature and skinny as a rail, as were far too many of the people living on farms during those hard times. She was part of a large family, but pitched in and did her share of the work by feeding and watering the family hogs to take labor from the shoulders of her father and brothers while they worked in the fields. She also helped care for the house, do the family washing and cooking and look out for her youngest brother who was still too small to do heavy farm work.

Like most young people of that day and this, she enjoyed socializing with friends and is remembered even today as a pretty young woman who drew the attention of potential suitors. Her cousins Dora King, Bessie King and Clara Bell Stanley lived nearby and the four often visited with each other. While the girls were cousins, they were so close that they often called each other "sister."[2]

Much of their conversation during the late summer of 1934 was likely about Lola's engagement to a young man in the community. She was, according to one acquaintance, "really excited and chattered about getting married like all young girls do." The Great Depression was then in its darkest days, but despite the hard times and hunger that stalked the land, the wedding was an exciting and anticipated event for the whole extended family.[3]

Like Academy Award winning actress Faye Dunaway, who was born nearby seven years after Lola's death, the young woman dreamed of escaping the hard life of the farm. She enjoyed visiting her sister and other relatives in Tallahassee where she saw in conveniences such as electric light, running water and well-stocked store shelves the promise of a better life away from the peanut and cotton fields of Jackson County. She hoped one day to live in Tallahassee, possibly even find a real job there and enjoy simple luxuries that must have seemed extravagant to a young woman from the farm.[4]

The Cannady family, like most of the other farm families of Jackson County, ate simple food and there was never enough of it. A cousin remembered meals of sweet potatoes and cornbread on visits to the weathered farmhouse. Protein was in short supply and pork chops, bacon and fried chicken were delicacies not often enjoyed. When flour could be afforded, especially after the crop came in or the season's hogs were sold, there were biscuits and gravy. Summer brought peaches and plums, and in the fall there were scuppernongs, ripe persimmons, and green boiled peanuts, along with sugar cane and cane syrup. All were anticipated the year round.[5]

Many modern writers proclaim 1934 as a time of great racism and say that tense racial relations prevailed in the Cannady neighborhood. This was not true. The Cannady family was on good terms with the African Americans of their community. Sallie Smith lived in a weather-beaten house just up the road and members of the Smith, Long and Neal families occupied similar homes scattered around the vicinity. The Smith home was a bustling place, not unlike the neighboring Cannady house. Smith shared her home with her recently widowed niece, Annie Smith, the mother of Claude Neal. Claude also lived in the old house, as did his common-law wife, his three-year-old daughter and a few other people.[6]

The Cannady and Smith/Neal families were friendly. George Cannady's children, including Lola, grew up playing and later working along-side members of Sallie Smith's extended family. Two of the Cannady daughters were about the same age as Claude Neal and knew him well. When he was named as a suspect in Lola's murder, her sister expressed shock and confusion at the allegation:

...I'd just like to see the man who did this just once. I can't understand what the motive was for this brutal deed. To think that Claude Neal, who had been raised with my sister and me and worked for us all his life, could do such a thing – it is unbelievable. I only wish that every resident of Jackson County could view the body of my sister.[7]

Neal helped George Cannady and his sons with heavy farm labor during the planting and picking seasons, while also maintaining fences and doing any other work George needed and could afford. The families lived very much alike. Their homes were weathered and sagging under the weight of the years, but the yards were swept clean of grass or weeds. They lived on cornbread and sweet potatoes, with a bit of pork or chicken thrown in now and then. Syrup, plums and scuppernongs were favorite sweets and they washed with lye soap made using the ashes from their fireplace. In the winter, cold wind blew through cracks in the walls and in the summer the heat was so intolerable that "siestas" were commonly taken on the front porch through the middle part of the day.[8]

Both families consisted of hard working people who were suffering through the greatest economic catastrophe that America had ever known. The debate over whether blacks or whites should receive government relief jobs might have been, and was, an issue in the towns, but out in the farm country there were no jobs to lead to such animosity. Race was, of course, an issue and it would be many years before desegregation finally brought the children of rural white families together with the children of rural black families for school. Black citizens generally did not vote, but most poor whites could not afford the poll tax and were also thus disenfranchised. Slang terms were commonly used by people of both races to refer to those of a different color. Such things were part of the "big picture" of life in the United States during the 1930s, but were not everyday concerns among the poor farm families of the Cannady neighborhood. People were just trying to keep food on their tables and survive to the next day.

One "piney woods philosopher" who grew up during the era of the Claude Neal lynching described the situation well when he pointed out that "Southern people back then were racist against blacks as a group. Northern people were racist against blacks as individuals." His point was that rural white Southerners in places like Jackson County tended to joke or speak in derogatory terms about African Americans as a race, but usually got along well with their black friends or with black neighbors that they knew and recognized. Northerners, on the other hand, spoke of the rights of African Americans as a race, but were prone to practice sometimes fearful and violent racism against individual black families or citizens that might, for example, try to move into their neighborhood.[9]

As the Cannady and Smith families went about their normal work in October of 1934, race was not at the top of their minds. It was harvest season or, as it is known in Jackson County to this day, "peanut picking time." Modern harvesting equipment had not yet been introduced, so farmers in those days pulled and shook the dirt from their peanut plants by hand, stacking them in tall piles. A "peanut picker" was then brought into the field and slowly moved from place to place. The peanut vines were forked into the picker which then plucked the peanuts themselves from the roots of the plants. It was not an efficient process and pounds of valuable nuts often were left behind. People then went over the fields by hand, picking up the peanuts that had fallen in the dirt and putting them into burlap bags. It was backbreaking labor.

Burlap bags, usually called "Croker sacks," were filled with peanuts until they were bursting at the seams and then thrown by hand into a mule-drawn wagon or onto the back of an early model Ford truck for the trip to the peanut mills in nearby Malone or Greenwood. The two small towns were vital centers of the 20th century peanut industry in Jackson County.

It is an interesting fact that Malone and Greenwood did not give the majority of their business to the county seat of Marianna, but instead shipped their crops north to Dothan, Alabama. This had been made possible in 1911 when the E.L. Marbury Lumber Company linked a series of former logging lines and opened the Alabama, Florida & Southern Railroad for business. By 1934 the AF&S had become the Alabama, Florida & Gulf (AF&G) and ran trains linking Greenwood to Malone and Malone to Cowarts, Alabama. The latter town was just east of Dothan and provided a connection with the Atlantic Coast Line Railroad, a competitor of the L&N which ran through Marianna.

The AF&G trains included both passenger and freight cars and the stations at Greenwood and Malone provided farmers and passengers with much easier access to rail transport than did the L&N at Marianna. The railroad connection also created a strong link between northern Jackson County and the growing Dothan area. Many of the key businesses in Malone were funded by investors from Dothan and a natural commercial and social alliance grew between the two communities. Not only did farmers like George Cannady carry their peanuts and cotton to the stations in Malone or Greenwood for shipment on the trains to Alabama, they could also take the train themselves. Dothan for them became a place where they could shop, visit the fair and enjoy the other attractions of a larger city. This key connection would play a large role in the events of October 1934.

October in Jackson County is a time of noticeable change in the seasons. The spectacular colors of more northern climes are not as noticeable, but the dogwoods, persimmons, sycamores and sweetgums do add a visual touch of fall to the landscape. The air cools noticeably and the first frost traditionally comes in the week or two before Halloween. It is still a busy month for farmers, with their crops coming in and the pressing need to finish up the season before the rains and freezes of winter. Unlike more southerly reaches of the state, Northwest Florida does experience some cold weather during the winter. Frosts and freezes are fairly common and even sleet and light snow fall from time to time.

October, then, is the busy month that comes before the real cold snaps of winter. It is the month when the smell of peanut dust is in the air. The dust rises so high into the atmosphere that it causes the sunsets to light up the western sky in glorious shades of red and orange. The oppressively hot weather of summer is gone and, while the afternoons are still warm, the mornings and the evenings begin to cool, sometimes even giving enough of a chill for local residents to reach for their jackets.

Besides the change in temperatures, there are other conditions that give October an almost perfect quality. It is the least rainy month of the year in Jackson County. Historically it rains on average only 4.5 days out of the 31 in October and the amount of rainfall in inches is the lowest of any month of the year. The humidity, which adds dramatically to the sweltering heat of summer, also drops. The days are often a perfect shade of blue and the rapid reduction in daylight hours causes trees, buildings and even flowers and shrubs to give off long shadows.

Autumn in Jackson County is a glorious time of year. Skies are sunny and the weather is cool and comfortable. But the arrival of fall in 1934 brought with it a time of brutal horror. The long shadows of that horrible time stretch across the Southern landscape to this day.

---

[1] Walter C. Jones, "Obama Administration Stands Up to Lynching Challenge," Friday, July 22, 2011, Online Athens; Interviews with current and former public officials of Jackson County, Florida, (names withheld by request).

[2] Testimony given by Dora King, Bessie King and Clara Bell Stanley in the Circuit Court for the Fourteenth Judicial Circuit, May 21, 1935.

[3] Interview with Friend of Lola Cannady, August 15, 2011 (name withheld by request).

[4] Interview with Cousin of Lola Cannady, November 28, 1999 (name withheld by request).

[5] *Ibid.*

[6] Interview with Cousin of Claude Neal, July 16, 1990 (name withheld by request).

[7] *Jackson County Floridan*, October 20, 1934, p.1.

[8] Interview with Cousin of Lola Cannady, November 28, 1999; Interview with cousin of Claude Neal, July 16, 1990; Testimony concerning such "siestas" was given by George Cannady in the Circuit Court for the Fourteenth Judicial Circuit, May 21, 1935.

[9] Interview with Bascom area resident, October 25, 2008 (name withheld by request).

CHAPTER TWO

The Murder of Lola Cannady

The morning of October 18, 1934, dawned sunny and beautiful in Jackson County. The skies were blue and the morning coolness gave the air a definite feel of fall. The Cannady family was up and moving before the sun that day. The women put together breakfast and gave one of the son's food to carry with him to the fields. Lola would stay home to watch out for the livestock and house, but other members of the family – including her mother and father – headed out early to visit their daughter in Tallahassee. The peanut money had come in and they were now taking a brief break from their labors to enjoy it. George Cannady even invested in a new mule.

Nineteen-year-old Lola Cannady spent the morning helping in the house. There was washing and cleaning to be done. The chickens had to be fed, the eggs collected and the cow milked. It took some time to get these chores done and out of the way, but by the middle of the day she had them pretty much done. Her younger brother – 12-year-old Raleigh - was at home with her and she told him that she was going to pump water for the hogs.

The hog pen was about one-quarter of a mile from the Cannady house, reached by a foot path that angled slightly to the southeast from the front of the east-facing house along the edge of a field and to the board pen where George Cannady kept his hogs. Lola had made the walk many times before and she undoubtedly enjoyed feeling the warmth of the sun on her face as

7

she walked through the cool air. Lola had no way of knowing it, but she was making the last walk of her life.

Another set of eyes was watching the young woman as she made her way idly along the path to the hog pen that morning. Whether she felt or sensed that she was being watched is not known. And how much she knew about the trouble that had broken out between her father and the Smith family in recent days also is a mystery. There definitely had been trouble, however, and the Cannady family believes to this day that it was the cause of the young woman's death.

The two older Cannady boys got into minor trouble in Malone. Alcohol was involved and Sallie Smith, who happened to be in town, reported them to the constable. The two were arrested on misdemeanor charges and an unhappy George Cannady was forced to go post their bail. The peanut and cotton money was not yet in and the family's finances were tight. Not only was George out hard cash, he was out a day of work from the boys.[1]

After getting back from Malone, George Cannady stewed about the incident, especially Smith's involvement in it. It took some time, but he finally let his anger boil over and went to the Smith house to confront Sallie Smith. He was out good money, he told her, and he wanted it back. She refused, telling him that she had no money. George, however, would not be turned away. An excitable man who believed in the old code of "an eye for an eye," he threw a rope around Sallie Smith's cow and led it away as repayment for his loss. It may have been the same cow that Lola Cannady milked on the morning of her death.[2]

It is difficult for people of the modern era to imagine the impact that the loss of a cow could have on a family in the Great Depression. Cows were sources of milk and the Smiths had small children in the home. Claude Neal's young daughter lived there and she was only three-years-old. Good milk cows were hard to come by and the loss of Sallie Smith's cow to George Cannady was no small matter. Anger simmered between the two families.

How much Lola knew about the confrontation between her father and Sallie Smith as she walked across the field that afternoon is not known. The topic must have been discussed around the Cannady home and not much could have been kept quiet considering the large size of the family and the small size of the house.

The woman may not have seen him at first, but as she made her way to the hog pen, someone else began making his way there too. Lola's older brother Wilford was working the new mule in a nearby field, trying to break it to the plow. Claude Neal had spent part of the morning helping him and was well known to him. Not long after Lola reached the hog pen, Wilford looked across the fields and saw his sister working at the pump. A man was there with her. George later mentioned what his son saw that day:

...My son was in the field about a quarter of a mile away when he saw someone talking with her at the pump, but he thought it was just one of the local boys and didn't pay much attention. He was right there in the field when she was being killed.[3]

Wilford Cannady was not able to identify the man he had seen talking to Lola because he had only glanced that way. He never heard his sister scream and never knew she was being raped and murdered, even though he was close enough to have saved her had he known what was happening. It was a knowledge that would burden him for the rest of his life.

Footprints would later be found leading from the scene and when traced, they led back to Sallie Smith's house. The footprints were those of a man and Claude Neal eventually admitted to authorities in Alabama that they were his. His was the only account anyone would ever hear of what happened to Lola Cannady.

In a statement to law enforcement officers and an attorney at the Escambia County Jail in Brewton, Alabama, Neal said that he spent the morning helping Wilford Cannady "break a mule to the plow." He left the field at around noon, picked up his common-law wife and child from her aunt's house, and went to the Smith house to see his mother. After seeing his mother, he told authorities, he went out into the field near the Cannady hog pen to look for a lost sow:

...Miss Lola Cannidy (sic.) was sitting by the pump cleaning out the hog trough.

She asked me if I would clean it out and I said that I would. I sat down and washed out the trough and then pumped it full of water for Miss Lola.[4]

The first time Neal confessed to authorities from Pensacola and Brewton, he told them his cousin Herbert Smith had been the instigator of the crime. He later admitted, however, that Smith had not been involved. Claude Neal then amended his confession by striking out any mentions of Smith. He had done the brutal deed himself, he told authorities.

In his original description of how the crime took place, however, a great deal of information is revealed as the reader realizes that Neal was using the person of Herbert Smith to channel an account of his own deeds:

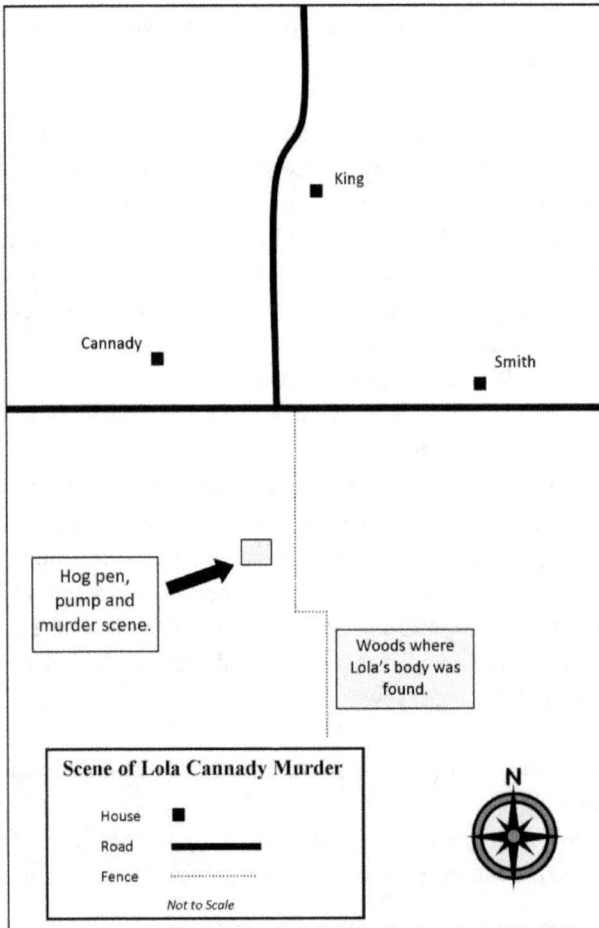

King

Cannady

Smith

Hog pen, pump and murder scene.

Woods where Lola's body was found.

Scene of Lola Cannady Murder

House ■

Road ▬▬▬

Fence ·······················

Not to Scale

N

When Miss Lola turned to go to the house, Herbert walked up and caught her by the arm. Herbert told her: "How about me being with you?" She said, "You must be a fool." Herbert said, "No, won't nobody know nothing about it." She told him to go ahead and go on, but Herbert pulled her by the arm and she started calling out for her brother, Mr. Willford. Herbert pulled her on over the fence about four or five steps away...Herbert choked her...and she stopped calling her brother.[5]

Neal said that Lola was dragged along a fence row for some distance before,"I had intercourse with her." He told authorities that he already knew the consequences of his actions, so a decision was made to "fix her where she won't tell nobody."[6]

Still using his cousin Herbert to channel his own actions, Claude Neal described the murder of Lola Cannady:

Herbert then broke down a little dead oak tree and broke off a piece about 3 or 3 ½ feet long and hit her in the head with it. She hadn't said anything from the time we made her lie down, and she breathed a few times after Herbert hit her in the head. Herbert dragged up a piece of log about five feet long and as big as my thigh up side of her and I dragged up another smaller piece and we laid them on her, or by the side of her. She was just breathing when we left her, she was not quite dead at that time.[7]

What Claude Neal did not tell in his confession was that even then the crime was far from over. He hinted as much when he said that Lola was "not quite dead at that time." This odd choice of words alone insinuates that there was another time.

The physical evidence found at the scene indicated to those searching for Lola Cannady on the night she disappeared that the murderer had gone back after her a second time. From footprints in the dirt of the field between the pump and Sallie Smith's house, the searchers could see that a man went back to the house but then came running back. Impressions in the ground near the hog pen showed that Lola Cannady was trying to drag herself over the fence. The murderer must have seen her and realized, as Neal said, that she was "not quite dead at that time." Panic stricken, the killer ran back to where she was, this time with a hammer in his hand. The young woman was dragged into a wooded area far back from the pump where the first attack

11

had taken place and her head was beaten in with the hammer. Lola breathed her last in tortured agony and the killer then had intercourse with her body.[8]

Claims have been made by some modern writers that Claude Neal killed Lola Cannady after she threatened to "tell the white people" on him for propositioning her. This is not true. The actual statement, according to an eyewitness who heard him confess after being arrested in Malone, was "I'll tell my daddy." There is great pathos in this warning, as in her time of greatest fear the young woman was thinking of her father, her protector. George Cannady loved his daughter like most fathers do and he never recovered emotionally from the fact that he was far away in Tallahassee and unable to help her that day.[9]

The rape and murder of Lola Cannady did not take place as easily as Neal described in his chilling confession. The first search parties came upon the scene of an enormous struggle. One man pointed out a large area in 1990 and described how tracks mixed with blood could be seen in circles in the dirt of the field. The young woman had fought desperately for her life before she was choked to unconsciousness, raped and bludgeoned.[10]

George Cannady told reporters in graphic terms that her body bore the marks of a vicious struggle:

...I can't get the picture of Lola out of my mind when we found her. Her throat was bruised and scratched where he had choked her so she couldn't cry out... Her head was beat in and she had been choked so hard her eyes were coming out of their sockets, her arms were broken and she was all beat up.[11]

Other eyewitnesses who saw Lola's body gave similar descriptions. They remembered that one of her legs was unnaturally bent and appeared to be broken. Her head was a misshapen mass that no longer resembled the laughing young woman of previous days. Her hands had been injured and broken in the fight to save herself from her murderer. There were bruises or marks on her thighs that looked like they had been caused by a man's hands.[12]

Some hours would pass before anyone realized that Lola was missing. Claude Neal told authorities a few days later that he went back to Sallie Smith's house where his wife and young daughter were waiting:

...I went to my mother's house and from there to my wife's aunt's place at Miss Rose Lewis's. I came back by Justice of the Peace Edgar Anderson's and talked to him.

I went back to my mother's and from there to Mr. John Daniel's. I was at Mr. Dave Daniel's house picking peas when the Sheriff came and got me.[13]

Several people told lawmen that they saw Neal on the afternoon of the murder and noticed that he had cuts and scratches on his hands. He told one that he had been in a fight and another that he had injured himself on a fence. The truth would soon become known.

---

[1] Interview with Cannady family member, December 23, 1995 (name withheld by request, hereafter Cannady family member #1); Interview with cousin of Claude Neal.

[2] *Ibid.*

[3] *Jackson County Floridan*, October 20, 1934, p. 1.

[4] Confession of Claude Neals, October 22, 1934, Governor Miller Papers, Alabama Department of Archives History (Copy from E.W. Carswell Collection).

[5] *Ibid.*

[6] *Ibid.*

[7] *Ibid.*

[8] Interview with Cannady family member #1; Interview with James King at crime scene, October 28, 1990 (hereafter King interview); Interview with Roy Beall, Sr., December 12, 1984 (hereafter Beall interview).

[9] Beall interview; Note: Cannady later experienced repeated emotional collapses as a result of his daughter's death.

[10] King interview.

[11] *Jackson County Floridan*, October 20, 1934, p. 1.

[12] King interview; Interview with eyewitness to crime scene, October 15, 1990 (name withheld by request, hereafter Eyewitness #2).

[13] Confession of Claude Neals, October 22, 1934.

CHAPTER THREE

The Search for Lola

Several hours passed before anyone noticed that Lola Cannady was missing. During this time Claude Neal – his clothes bloody and his hand badly cut - came back home to Sallie Smith's house. His common law wife and three-year-old daughter were there, as were his mother, Annie "Kitty" Smith, and his great-aunt Sallie "Sal" Smith. The women knew that something awful had happened and quickly tried to hide evidence of the crime. Claude changed out of his bloody and torn clothing and the women began trying to wash out the blood stains. He stayed only a short time, but one family member remembers seeing him hiding beneath the house.[1]

As the afternoon passed and concern grew over Lola's whereabouts, members of her family went out to the hog pen to look for her. When they got there they found troubling signs of foul play. Not only could Lola not be found, but there was the area in the dirt where a man and a woman had obviously waged a fierce battle.[2]

As darkness fell, the search became more frantic. Word now spread throughout the area and families poured to the Cannady farm to help. One participant remembered that cars lined the full 80 acre field and woodlot where the search was focused and were parked along both sides of the dirt road from the Cannady place all the way out to State Highway 71.[3]

As the search for Lola intensified, one of Claude Neal's cousins walked the mile or so up the dirt road from her house to visit the family. She got there and found her aunt Sallie trying to wash blood from a man's clothes. When she asked what had happened, the young woman was told, "Claude done killed that white girl." Terrified, she ran home as fast as she could. She recalled seeing numerous cars heading for the Cannady place as she fled the Smith house.[4]

The search, meanwhile, expanded out into the fields that surrounded the farm. One participant remembered that men walked the ground ten feet apart in parallel rows, looking for either Lola or some clue of what had happened to her. It did not take them long to find a man's footprints leading from the area of the water pump across the open field to and from Sallie Smith's house. The home was clearly visible in the distance from the pump area. Other tracks were found leading from the area of the hog pen along a north-south fence row that led back to the wooded area on land owned by Sallie Smith.

This second set of tracks attracted immediate attention because they appeared to be those of both a man and a woman. Something was wrong, however, with the look of the woman's tracks. An eyewitness recalled that the female did not appear to have been walking on her own and that her trail was made up mostly of drag marks mixed with occasional footprints. The other set of prints were those of a man and looked identical to those found leading across the field to and from Sallie Smith's house. The tracks disappeared from view as they entered the leaves and pine straw of the woodlot.[5]

Darkness fell but torches and lanterns illuminated the way as the men continued their desperate search for Lola. Their family members set up camp in the fields around the Cannady house, building fires to provide warmth and cook a little food. A neighbor recalled that the entire 80 acre tract between the house and the hog pen was illuminated by the fires.[6]

A small group of men followed the male footprints from the pump area to Sallie Smith's house, where they found her at home with Claude Neal's common law wife, his three year old daughter and some of his younger siblings. As one of Neal's cousins had already seen, the women were trying to wash a man's bloody clothes and were still trying to do so when the collection of neighbors arrived at the house. The clothes were those of a grown man and the only grown man then living in the house was Claude

Neal, but he was nowhere to be found. Word spread quickly that he had been implicated in the disappearance of Lola Cannady. The news was passed house to house and farm to farm in those days when telephone service did not exist in the rural areas of Jackson County. By the next morning, Neal's possible involvement in whatever had happened to Lola was common knowledge in nearby Malone.[7]

The search went on all night and fears over Lola's safety grew proportionately. By early morning it was clear that a major crime had taken place and as daylight broke, someone from the Cannady farm made their way to nearby Greenwood to call the sheriff. Telephone lines had not then been run into the rural areas of Jackson County.

Although many modern writers have claimed that Jackson County Sheriff W.F. "Flake" Chambliss did not investigate the lynching of Claude Neal, he actually filed a seven page written report with Governor Dave Sholtz on October 31, 1934. According to that report, he received a call notifying him that Lola Cannady was missing at 6 a.m. on the morning of Friday, October 19th. He started immediately for the scene.[8]

Chambliss drove the most popular vehicle of his day, a Model A Ford. While the car was capable of doing a top speed of 65 miles per hour, the roads of Jackson County didn't make such speeds feasible. Even so, the sheriff kept the "pedal to the medal" and reached the Cannady farm in about 45 minutes.[9]

Before he got there, however, the searchers made a dreadful discovery. Lola's body was found deep in the woodlot by her uncle and cousin, both of whom were members of the King family. She had been beaten to death and her body then covered with logs and pine limbs. The young woman appeared to have been dead for a number of hours.[10]

Flake Chambliss had just arrived by the gate at the Cannady house when news came across the fields that a body had been found. The sheriff went directly to the scene, where he reported that he saw Lola's body at 6:45 a.m. and found what appeared to be a piece of cloth from a man's shirtsleeve. Under Chambliss' direction, a search for additional evidence was conducted in the area where the body had been found.[11]

It was the practice in those days for a coroner's inquest to be held over the bodies of murder victims. The duties of coroner were part of the responsibilities of the county judge, but Judge Oswald was then in Quincy for a dog show. A justice of the peace was assigned to head the investigation and a panel was quickly assembled at the murder scene. Dr.

George S. Hodges, who routinely examined bodies for coroner's inquests in Jackson County, was notified and asked to come immediately to the scene. Meanwhile, a local farmer made an important discovery near the logs where Lola's body was found.[12]

Johnny Hatcher had been assisting in the search for evidence when he found "a string with the loop and stem of a watch." He pointed it out to Sheriff Chambliss, who added it to the growing body of physical evidence in the murder. The watch stem would soon prove critical in connecting Claude Neal to the crime. For unexplained reasons, historian James R. McGovern downplayed Hatcher's discovery in his 1982 book, *Anatomy of a Lynching: The Killing of Claude Neal*. He deemed it and other evidence in the case, "less than persuasive."[13]

McGovern asserted that the rings on pocket watches were "generally standard, after all," but provided no documentation to support this claim. He also neglected to mention that the evidence actually consisted of the entire broken stem of a man's watch and not just a "ring." Why the historian withheld critical information about the evidence is not explained in his book, but it is possible that he may not have known the actual facts. McGovern and his researcher spent very limited time in the rural areas of Jackson County trying to talk to people who remembered the lynching. For book research into a topic about which eyewitnesses were still living, their effort was minimal at best. The professor apparently did not talk to family members of either Johnny Hatcher, who discovered the watch parts, or Phil Coulliette, the deputy sheriff that arrested Claude Neal.[14]

McGovern also downplayed or did not learn of other evidence recovered at the scene. The blood-stained piece of a shirt found near Lola Cannady's body by Sheriff Chambliss, for example, he described as "not fully convincing," while admitting at the same time that it "warranted careful scrutiny." The professor also pointed out that no effort was made to recover fingerprints from the murder weapon but did not mention that fingerprint comparison was still a very new crime solving technique in the United States and had not yet spread down to rural law enforcement agencies. Congress, in fact, had only authorized the Federal Bureau of Investigation to begin building its fingerprint library and working directly with fingerprints in 1924. F.B.I. agents had been placing heavy emphasis on fingerprint comparisons for less than ten years and fingerprint records would not be used to successfully prosecute a case against a habitual offender until 1938, four years after the murder of Lola Cannady. It was not until 1939 that the use of fingerprint analysis to identify bodies following the U.S.S. *Squalus* disaster provided convincing proof to the public at large of the value of such evidence.[15]

The sheriff's failure to use technology not yet available to him aside, he did assemble an impressive amount of physical evidence at and near the scene of the murder. All of it pointed to Claude Neal as the prime suspect in the case.

At 9:30 a.m., Dr. Hodges arrived on the scene and examined the body as part of the coroner's inquest. He found that Lola had been raped and murdered and that her body was bruised and lacerated. This determination was confirmed a short time later by George Cannady, who told reporters that his daughter's "head was beat in and she had been choked so hard her eyes were coming out of their sockets, her arms were broken and she was all beat up." As has been noted, Mr. Cannady also said that Lola's "throat was bruised and scratched where he had choked her so she couldn't cry out."[16]

The examination of the body complete, Lola's family was allowed to take her home to prepare her for burial. The grieving parents offered the last tender care they could to the body of their daughter. The women of the family washed her as well as they could and dressed the body for burial, while the men arranged for a wooden coffin.

Sheriff Chambliss crossed the field to Sallie Smith's house while the family cared for Lola's body. There he saw Neal's wet and bloodstained clothes, which he took into evidence. Sallie Smith was arrested as an accessory to the crime. Outrage was already beginning to grow in the neighborhood and the sheriff had Smith taken directly to the Washington County Jail in Chipley. The Jackson County Jail in Marianna had recently been called a less than secure facility by the county grand jury and it was felt the woman would be safer in the Chipley jail.[17]

As the investigation continued at the Cannady farm, Deputy Phil Coulliette and Constable Sim Hall found Claude Neal in Malone and took him into custody. He did not resist arrest and when he was searched for weapons, Coulliette removed the suspect's watch from his pocket and noticed that it was missing its stem and ring. The deputy also noted that Neal's hands were badly scratched and cut. The young man was arrested for suspicion of involvement in the murder of Lola Cannady.[18]

Deputy Coulliette and Constable Hall took Neal into Beall's store in Malone. A legendary basketball coach and businessman, store operator Roy

Beall, Sr., would go on to serve more than five decades on the Jackson County School Board. He was present that morning when Coulliette and Hall brought Neal into the store and asked to use his telephone. Deputies in those days did not have two-way radios and had to rely on telephones that were few and far between to communicate with the main office in Marianna. Beall gave his permission and Coulliette called Marianna to report that he had arrested Claude Neal. Officers there informed him that the sheriff was at the Cannady farm.[19]

Roy Beall was interviewed about the incident fifty years later and retained a vivid memory of what he had seen and heard that morning. Claude Neal was familiar to him and Beall recalled that he asked the young man, "Claude, did you do this thing?" Neal, he said, responded with a simple, "Yes, sir." Beall then asked, "Why did you do it?" He remembered with a shiver that Neal looked at his own hands and then replied with the chilling statement, "The Devil was in me." Beall also recalled noticing that Neal's hands were badly cut and scratched.[20]

Placed in handcuffs, Claude Neal was taken out of the store and put in the backseat of Coulliette's Model A Ford. A crowd of local citizens watched in silence. Unsure of what to do and with no way to communicate directly with the sheriff, the deputy took his suspect south from Malone to the Cannady farm. The officer did not know that a sense of outrage and anger was already building among the people gathered there.[21]

---

[1] Interview with Neal family member.
[2] King and Hatcher interviews.
[3] *Ibid.*
[4] Interview with Neal cousin.
[5] King interview.
[6] *Ibid.*
[7] *Ibid.*
[8] W.F. Chambiss, Report on the Lynching of Claude Neal, October 31, 1934 (hereafter Chambliss, Lynching Report).
[9] *Ibid.*
[10] King interview.
[11] *Ibid.*; Chambliss, Lynching Report.
[12] Chambliss, Lynching Report; Hatcher interview.

[13] James R. McGovern, *Anatomy of a Lynching: The Killing of Claude Neal*, Baton Rouge, p. 45.

[14] *Ibid.*, pp. 45-46.

[15] *Ibid.*; Jeffrey G. Barnes, "History," *The Fingerprint Sourcebook*, U.S. Department of Justice, Chapter One, pp. 4-22.

[16] *Jackson County Floridan*, October 20, 1934, p. 1.

[17] King interview; Chambliss, Lynching Report.

[18] Chambliss, Lynching Report; Beall interview; Hatcher interview; Interview with family member of Deputy Phil Coulliette, July 28, 1984 (name withheld by request, hereafter referred to as Coulliette Family Member).

[19] Beall interview; Coulliette Family Member.

[20] Beall interview.

[21] *Ibid.*; Coulliette Family Member; King interview.

CHAPTER FOUR

The Effort to Protect Claude Neal

At around 9 o'clock on the morning of October 19, 1934, Deputy Sheriff Phil Coulliette arrived at the Cannady farm. A terrified Claude Neal was handcuffed and in the backseat of his car. The crowd at the farm had grown dramatically and news of the brutal murder of Lola Cannady was still spreading like wildfire through the fields and pine woods of northeastern Jackson County.

Sheriff Chambliss spoke briefly with the suspect, but gained nothing useful from him. Neal had admitted his involvement in the crime to Roy Beall, Sr., earlier in the morning, but as soon as he saw the size and anger of the crowd at the Cannady farm he wasted no time in proclaiming his innocence. An eyewitness recalled years later the sound of the suspect's voice as he repeatedly denied any knowledge of the murder. He was, according to the quite believable account, "very much afraid."[1]

Realizing that a hostile situation was developing around him, the sheriff ordered Deputy Coulliette to take Neal immediately to Marianna and from there as fast as possible to Chipley. The deputy did so, leaving the items taken from the suspect at the time of his arrest – including the broken pocket watch – at the sheriff's office on the second floor of the Jackson County Courthouse before he and Neal continued on to Chipley.[2]

At 12 noon, the body of Lola Cannady was quickly examined by Dr. A.D. MacKinnon of Marianna. Sheriff Chambliss and State Attorney John Carter had asked him to go to the farm to offer an additional opinion on the state of the body. His observations, which were recorded only second hand, remain controversial to this day.[3]

Dr. Hodges, it will be recalled, had examined the body that morning shortly after it was found. He reported to the coroner's jury that Lola had been raped and murdered and that her remains showed evidence of both bruises and lacerations. Dr. MacKinnon reported, however, that "no signs of rape appear, but that she had had intercourse." He also noted that he saw "no bruises or lascerations."[4]

This statement by Dr. MacKinnon is exceedingly strange, considering that Lola's head had been beaten in with a blunt object. George Cannady told reporters that his daughter's arms were broken and that scrapes and scratches were visible on her neck where she had been choked by her assailant. Other eyewitnesses independently verified this, as did one of Lola's sisters. As might be expected, Dr. MacKinnon's observations have sparked controversy over the eight decades that have passed since the murder.

A likely explanation for the difference in the statements of the two doctors is that Dr. MacKinnon did not see Lola's body at around 12 noon on the 19th. She had been dead for nearly 24 hours by that point and her body had not been embalmed or refrigerated. The decomposition process would have been progressing rapidly. In addition, Dr. MacKinnon saw the body after it had been washed by Lola's family and prepared for burial. Blood from her wounds had been washed away as had other physical evidence. Combined with changes due to decomposition, bruises and scratches seen earlier in the day by Dr. Hodges might not have been as visible by the time of Dr. MacKinnon's brief examination.

MacKinnon's statement that he found evidence that Lola had engaged in intercourse, but saw no signs of rape, has been the subject of much confusion over the years. Many modern writers have seized on this observation as proof for a theory that Claude Neal and Lola Cannady were having a relationship, even though this theory did not surface until after both were dead and was proposed by individuals who knew neither of them. Not a single person that actually knew ether Lola or Claude claimed that there had been a relationship between them.

In fact, Dr. MacKinnon's observations were not necessarily at odds with those of Dr. Hodges. The washing of Lola's body might well have eliminated indications that she had been raped. In addition, Claude Neal said in his subsequent confessions that Lola had been choked until she was unconscious before he had intercourse with her. This, of course, could explain why Dr. MacKinnon did not find evidence of force.[5]

Another and much darker possibility regarding Dr. MacKinnon's examination is that Lola was already dead when her body was sexually assaulted the second time. The young woman had been choked until she was unconscious and severely beaten, then dragged into the woods and beaten again. Neal later could say only that he "thought" she was still breathing at that time. The allegation that Lola Cannady's body was sexually abused after her death has been a closely guarded secret in northeastern Jackson County for nearly 80 years. The belief that this was true, however, contributed greatly to the decision by a group of local men that Claude Neal should be lynched.[6]

Murder investigations often involve the questioning of several potential suspects as law enforcement officers try to interpret the evidence available to them. When blood-stained and wet clothes were found at Sallie Smith's home that morning, some of her family members claimed that these items had been brought there for washing by a white man. Sheriff Chambliss spoke with this individual, Calvin Cross, at 3 p.m. on the 19th and was able to locate witnesses who confirmed that Cross had been nowhere near the scene when Lola was killed. The man was absolved of any involvement in the crime.[7]

At 4 p.m. on the same day that her body was found in Sallie Smith's woodlot, Lola Cannady was laid to rest in the little cemetery by the white frame Baptist church in Bascom. She had been a member there and a large crowd was in attendance, although it is not believed that any reporters were present. It is not known whether Sheriff Chambliss attended, but it is likely that he did. He was at Sallie Smith's nearby house just one hour later when he arrested Claude Neal's mother, Annie Smith on suspicion of being an accessory to murder.[8]

The situation in Jackson County was growing more unsettled by the hour and the sheriff knew it. He had already had both Claude Neal and Sallie Smith taken to the jail in Chipley for their safety and now did the same with Neal's mother. By the time she arrived in Washington County,

Claude was already gone. He had only been there for one hour when rumors of a forming lynch mob forced Chambliss to ask Sheriff John Harrell to have him moved on to the even more secure Bay County Jail in Panama City.[9]

That evening at the courthouse in Marianna, Sheriff Chambliss, State Attorney Carter and the members of the coroner's jury reviewed the physical evidence that had been collected throughout the day. The clothing that had been seized from Sallie Smith's house and which was thought to belong to Claude Neal was examined. It was noticed that one of the sleeves on the bloody shirt seized at the Smith house was torn. The bloodstained piece of cloth found near Lola Cannady's body was produced and was found to be a perfect match.[10]

The pocket watch found in Neal's pocket at the time of his arrest was also examined and compared with the broken watch stem and loop found at the murder scene. The stem from Neal's watch was found to be missing and the watch stem found near Lola's body turned out to be a perfect match.[11]

Other evidence discussed that night included the cuts on Neal's hands, which appeared consistent with the blood evidence and a small piece of skin found on a fence near the murder scene. The footprint patterns found at the scene showed that someone had gone back and forth from the murder scene to the Smith house. Statements taken by the sheriff and coroner's jury members at the scene indicated that witnesses had seen a man talking to Lola Cannady shortly before her death and that Claude Neal had left his home and gone into the field at the time of Lola's disappearance. Sheriff Chambliss had also found a bloody hammer hidden beneath the Smith house. The evidence pointed almost exclusively to Claude Neal, but the investigation did not stop with his emergence as the key suspect.

While this deliberative review and discussion of the evidence was underway at the Jackson County Courthouse, an entirely different scene took place in the rural countryside of northeastern Jackson County. News of the brutal nature of Lola's murder had spread quickly, as did the knowledge that Claude Neal was the primary suspect in the crime. Passions ran very high among the people gathered in the fields around the Cannady home and at some point late in the day a group of around 100 men gathered to discuss what should be done.

Many of these men had served during World War I and the organization they formed was deliberate and disciplined. They would employ military-like tactics over coming days and by doing so confounded the best efforts of law enforcement to keep Claude Neal safe and out of their hands. While some modern writers have claimed otherwise, these men did not comprise a wild and drunken mob. Those who saw them said, in fact, that they were sober, grim and determined.

The organization coalesced around a central core of 15 leaders, all of whom were well-known in the area. Under their direction, information was compartmentalized to help assure operational security. There was little if any disagreement among them. Claude Neal, they believed, should die. They were convinced that Neal had committed a crime so brutal that he was undeserving of the niceties of the judicial system. Almost to a man they agreed that Claude Neal should be taken from jail, brought to the Cannady farm and turned over to George Cannady to do with as he saw fit.[12]

One man at the farm that afternoon, however, had the courage to disagree. Anderson Bowles was the Clerk of Courts for Jackson County and had stopped at the Cannady home to pay his respects. He learned that a lynch mob was forming and determined to do what he could to stop it in its tracks. With no way to contact the sheriff and no support from anyone else in the crowd, he climbed into the bed of a pickup truck and called out to the growing mob.[13]

Often known by his unique nickname of "Candy," Anderson Bowles was a respected figure in Jackson County. The son of a veteran of the Battle of Marianna, he was elected county clerk of courts in 1906 and held that position until he was elected sheriff in 1912. He served as sheriff until 1916, when he was defeated for reelection by A.J. Lewis. Bowles then remained out of public life until 1928 when he ran for his old job as clerk of courts and was returned to the position by the voters of Jackson County. He was two years into his second term when Lola Cannady was murdered in 1934.

According to an eyewitness at the farm that evening, Bowles begged the men with the words "Don't do it." He told them that lynching Neal "was murder" and urged that the sheriff and court system be allowed to handle the matter. While one or two of those present might have taken his words to heart and slipped away, Bowles' pleas by and large fell on deaf ears.[14]

Shortly after nightfall the men at the farm headed out in a caravan of 29 cars and trucks. Deputy Dave Ham was in Cottondale at 7:30 p.m. when they arrived there. Concerned by what he was seeing, he called Sheriff Chambliss to report that "suspicious looking cars are passing through Cottondale going toward Chipley and Panama City." The sheriff phoned

27

Sheriff H.O. Hobbs in Panama City, urging him to "move Neal to Pensacola or some other safe place because (the) mob is on the way to get him." A warning call also was placed to Sheriff Harrell in Chipley and in both cities officers moved into action.[15]

Chipley's jail was relatively strong and Sheriff Harrell made sure that Sallie and Annie Smith were behind strong iron doors in his safest cell. The mob reached the Washington County Jail not 30 minutes after Deputy Ham saw it passing through Cottondale. With tear gas bombs ready in case he and his men had to repel an attack, Harrell spoke to the men and told them that Neal had been at his jail earlier in the day but was no longer there. He further told them he did not know where the suspect had been taken, but that it was undoubtedly to a secure location. The men were primarily looking for Neal at this point and left without attempting to seize the two women.[16]

In Panama City, meanwhile, Sheriff Hobbs and his men quickly took steps to move Neal to safety. At 9:10 p.m. the sheriff and three deputies loaded Claude into a car and carried him to the waterfront where he was placed on a boat. That vessel then set sail for Camp Walton (today's Fort Walton Beach). As events quickly proved, there had not been a minute to spare:

The mob of over 100, in 27 cars, unmasked, composed largely of farmers, reached Panama City at 9:30 and went directly to the jail demanding the negro. Jailer Will Pledger told them that Sheriff Hobbs had left with the negro and he did not know where they were headed for. Jailer Pledger allowed leaders of the mob to make a complete search of the jail and premises.[17]

Sadly, while he was not hurt by the men from Jackson County that night, Will Pledger gave his life in the line of duty just one year later. He was killed in September 1935 while trying to arrest two suspects in another crime.

Despite being allowed to search the jail and not finding Neal there, the men from Jackson County did not immediately leave:

When the negro was not found, the crowd still waited around the jail. Sheriff Hobbs had returned then and explained to the crowd that he had been requested to remove the negro by the officers of Jackson county, and that the negro was then out of Bay county. He asked the men kindly to disperse and expressed deepest sympathy for them.[18]

While the sheriff watched from inside the jail, the men gathered outside in small groups, apparently deciding what they should do next. At 11:30 p.m., they finally left Panama City in detachments. Some went to Wewahitchka in Gulf County to see if Neal was in the jail there. Others spread out through the countryside looking for him at various convict camps.[19]

A reporter for the *Panama City Pilot* newspaper saw the mob and spoke with some of its members that night:

The crowd of Jackson countians were orderly, quiet and determined, talking in undertones. None were masked. There was no display of arms, no boisterousness. They were 100 men determined to defend womanhood against a crime charged that is worse than murder.[20]

Having barely escaped the hands of the mob at Panama City, Claude Neal was carried by water to Camp Walton where he arrived early the next morning. Immediately placed into a car, he was driven to Pensacola where he was turned over to Sheriff H.E. Gandy at the Escambia County Jail.[21]

---

[1] King interview.

[2] Chambliss, Lynching Report; Coulliette Family Member.

[3] Chabliss, Lynching Report.

[4] *Ibid.*

[5] Confession of Claude Neals, October 25, 1934; Second Confession of Claude Neal.

[6] Interviews with multiple eyewitnesses and family members of other eyewitnesses, 1983, 1986 and 2011 (names withheld by request).

[7] Chambliss, Lynching Report; Coulliette Family Member.

[8] Chambliss, Lynching Report.

[9] *Ibid.*

[10] *Ibid.*

[11] *Ibid.*

[12] Interviews with Lynch Mob Members #1 and #2 (names withheld).

[13] Hatcher interview.

[14] *Ibid.*

[15] Chambliss, Lynching Report.

[16] Report dated Chipley, October 20, appearing in the *Seattle Daily Times*, October 21, 1934, p. 4.

[17] *Panama City Pilot*, October 25, 1934, p. 1.

[18] *Ibid.*

[19] *Ibid.*

[20] *Ibid.*

[21] Chambliss, Lynching Report.

CHAPTER FIVE

The Confession of Claude Neal

Friday, October 19th, had been a long day for Jackson County's exhausted sheriff. He had been called to the Cannady farm at 6:30 Friday morning and was still in his office at the courthouse after midnight, the long hours made worse by the day he had spent dealing with a brutal murder and the tension of a growing vigilante sentiment. Saturday would be no better.

Flake Chambliss had only been in bed for an hour or two when he was awakened by the mob. He later reported to Governor Dave Sholtz that at 2:30 a.m. on Saturday, October 20th, a "crowd of around 50 people (came) to the Sheriff's house and (de)manded to know whereabouts of Neal, but information (was) refused."[1]

The position of Sheriff Chambliss with regard to the mob has been wildly misstated by many modern writers. Jackson County was primarily a rural county during the Great Depression and the men making up the group determined to lynch Claude Neal were the sheriff's friends, neighbors and probably even relatives. The brutal nature of Lola Cannady's murder had feelings running high and many citizens supported the statements and objectives of the mob, whether they said so publicly or not. Others, of course, did not and it is impossible now to say which group was in the majority. But for those who believed Neal should be taken from jail and

31

turned over to George Cannady, Flake Chambliss rapidly became the man they blamed for denying them that opportunity.

During the week that passed between Claude Neal's arrest and his kidnapping from an Alabama jail by the lynch mob, Sheriff Chambliss did everything in his power to protect the man and give him his day in court. The sheriff faced down mob members at his own home and did everything possible to keep not only Neal, but the suspect's mother and great aunt one step ahead of an extremely organized group of men that left no stone unturned in its effort to find them.

Despite his efforts, Flake Chambliss' reputation has been savaged by many modern writers. A typical example is "The Ballad of Claude Neal," written in 2010, which claims that after Neal was arrested, "a confession was beaten out of him by the sheriff's department in Greenwood, Florida." In reality, Neal was in the hands of the Jackson County Sheriff's Department (which did not have an office in Greenwood) for less than one hour and during that time gave no confession to the crime. Not a single shred of evidence has ever been presented to suggest that Sheriff Chambliss or his deputies raised so much as a finger against their prisoner.[2]

Even though the claim that Chambliss and his deputies beat Claude Neal was completely false, it made it to the floor of the U.S. Senate in 2005 when Senator Mary Landrieu, a Louisiana Democrat, claimed that, "After 10 hours of torture, Claude Neal (quote) "confessed" to the murder of a girl with whom he was allegedly having an affair. For his safety, he was transferred to an Alabama prison." The senator's speech was in support of the passage of a non-binding resolution by the U.S. Senate apologizing for that body's failure to pass a national anti-lynching bill during the 1930s. Unfortunately, Senator Landrieu repeated the torture story about the Jackson County Sheriff's Office with no regard for its truth. Neal was not tortured in Jackson County and spent only about one hour, not ten, in the hands of Sheriff Chambliss and his deputies.[3]

The truth about Sheriff Chambliss is that, despite strong hostility from many of his constituents, he worked diligently not only to investigate the murder of Lola Cannady, but to protect Claude Neal and the two Smith women. By 10 a.m. on Saturday, October 20th, for example, he and State Attorney John Carter were in Chipley questioning Sallie and Annie Smith.[4]

The interview was interrupted when the members of the lynch mob suddenly appeared outside the Washington County Jail. This time the men were after the two Smith women and demanded them from the jailor. For the second time in less than ten hours, Chambliss confronted them. He talked to the leaders of the mob and calmly but deliberately persuaded them to leave. They did as he asked, but threatened to come back.[5]

Whether the questioning of the two women continued after the incident with the mob is not known. The sheriff was back in Marianna by 4:30 p.m. There he received his third and perhaps strangest communication from the lynch mob:

4:30 P.M: Proposition to Sheriff that if he will cut down size of guard transporting Neal after conviction mob would probably let him be brought to trial, flatly refused.[6]

How this proposal was delivered is not known. Sheriff Chambliss may have elaborated in his verbal report to Governor Sholtz, but his written report did not include more detail and the case files associated with the murder of Lola Cannady and lynching of Claude Neal disappeared from the Jackson County Courthouse in Marianna decades ago.

The mob, meanwhile, lived up to its threat to return to the Chipley jail. At 10:30 a.m. on Sunday morning (October 21st), Sheriff John Harrell telephoned Deputy Walter Davis in Marianna to report that men from Jackson County had returned to his jail, "demanding the two Smith women." He again turned them away, but was warned by them that they "were coming back with torches to cut into the jail."[7]

Sheriff Chamblis and Deputy Davis immediately set out by car for Chipley. They met briefly with Sheriff Harrell to learn the details of the latest confrontation with the mob and Chambliss then went back into the cells to talk with the two women. Whether from fear that they would be lynched by the mob for the actions of Neal or from a night of reflection, they decided to tell the lawman what had happened in their home at the time Lola Cannady was killed.

Sallie Smith admitted to Sheriff Chambliss that Neal had left her house after the noon meal and that she had seen him approach Lola Cannady and then heard the young woman scream. Her grand-nephew was gone about two hours, she said, but had come back with his clothes stained with blood.[8]

Annie Smith, identified with her nickname of "Kitten" by the sheriff, confirmed Sallie's statements and further admitted "washing Neal's clothes after he came back to the house from the field." There was, she said, "blood on (his) clothes."[9]

The statements of the two women gave the Jackson County officers a major break in their investigation. They now had independent confirmation from Claude Neal's own mother that the bloody clothes and especially the torn shirt found at the Smith house belonged to him. Since the blood-stained piece of cloth found with Lola's body came from that shirt, they now had compelling physical evidence linking Neal to the murder, as well as a firm chain of custody for that evidence. In addition, Sallie Smith's statement provided a chilling link between Claude Neal and Lola Cannady on the day of the murder and, in particular, with her screams.

Combined with the discovery of the bloody hammer at the Smith house, the recovery of the stem and loop from Neal's watch near Lola's body and the cuts on his hands, the case against Claude Neal was now solid. While Sheriff Chambliss did not have a confession from the suspect himself, he had more than sufficient evidence to take the case to trial. Many modern murder cases end in convictions based on far less compelling evidence.

The sheriff took statements from the two women and then sent Deputy Davis on the road with them heading west. Sheriff Gandy of Escambia County agreed to house them at the jail in Pensacola, where Claude Neal earlier had been taken. All of the officers believed that putting the two women in jail in the larger city would assure their protection from the mob.

Unfortunately for Claude Neal, the press now became his worst enemy. The sensational news from Jackson and surrounding counties was electrifying. With readers hungry for more and more detail about the situation, the wire services began providing a steady stream of updates. These included the latest rumors on the whereabouts of the three suspects.

By Monday morning (October 22nd), for example, newspapers across the nation carried stories datelined Chipley that reported the two women had been removed from the Washington County Jail on Sunday afternoon and carried to Pensacola. Such updates provided detail for readers, but also proved to be a critical source of information for the leaders of the mob as they continued their efforts to learn the whereabouts of Claude Neal, his mother and great aunt.[10]

The morning of Monday, October 22nd, began with a flurry of activity at the Jackson County Courthouse in Marianna when the coroner's jury announced the completion of its investigation of Lola's death. The young woman, the jury ruled, had been brutally raped and murdered by Claude Neal. The coroner's inquest report and evidence was turned over to State Attorney John Carter. Circuit court was convened at 9 a.m. and Judge Amos Lewis ordered the Jackson County Grand Jury to re-convene on Wednesday morning to consider indictments in the case. Summons were issued to potential grand jurors.[11]

Even as Judge Lewis gaveled the circuit court session to order, Sheriff Chambliss received an unexpected call from Sheriff Gandy in Pensacola. Claude Neal, the latter officer reported, had made a "complete confession and implicated a negro named Herbert Smith of Malone." Gandy asked Chambliss to "arrest Smith and bring him to Pensacola to confront Neal." The sheriff reported that he "immediately made investigation and located Smith."[12]

From the Escambia County sheriff, Chambliss learned that Claude Neal was no longer in Pensacola but had been moved across the state line to Brewton, Alabama. The jail there was thought to be even more secure and the location had not been mentioned in any of the newspaper reports. The Jackson County sheriff urged Gandy by both phone and wire not to let Neal sign a written confession "implicating Herbert Smith until confronted by Smith and further investigation is made here." Gandy replied that he was convinced that Smith had been implicated in the crime and urged Chambliss to make the arrest and bring Smith to Pensacola that night so he could confront Neal.[13]

Sheriff Chambliss was extremely cautious about Neal's sudden implication of a second suspect in the crime and for good reason. Neither the physical evidence nor the testimony of witnesses gave any indication that more than one person had been involved in the murder. Sallie and Annie Smith had made no mention of seeing a second man that day and the searchers had found only one set of male footprints at the scene while looking for Lola, the ones that had been followed back to Sallie Smith's house.

At 10 a.m., Sheriff Chambliss asked Deputy Coulliette to investigate the whereabouts of Herbert Smith on the day of the murder. If he found reason to be suspicious of the man's movements, Coulliette was to notify the sheriff and the two would coordinate their movements so that Chambliss could pick him up "at dark and take him to Pensacola without (the) knowledge of the people." As this effort to investigate Herbert Smith stepped into high gear, a different drama began to unfold in circuit court.[14]

1934 was the year of the bank robbers. It had begun with Bonnie and Clyde continuing their murderous rampage through Texas, Oklahoma and Louisiana. John Dillinger, on the run from law enforcement, attended Cubs games in Chicago. "Baby Face" Nelson led police officers on a bloody trail of death. "Pretty Boy" Floyd, the Oklahoma outlaw, was on the run in Ohio. "Machine Gun" Kelly was settling in to spend the rest of his life in the new maximum security prison at Alcatraz, a facility that opened its doors for the first time that same year. It was, as historians have noted, the "heyday of the Depression-era bank robbers."

The activities of these and other notorious outlaws inspired desperate gangs of "wannabe" bank robbers. In August, just a few miles from the Cannady farm, one such group took the first step on what its members thought would be a chance to live the high life while robbing banks from coast to coast.

The planned crime spree began near Malone on the morning of August 21, 1934, when M.F. Dudley ordered an African American farmhand named Willie Reece to drive Buford Mears and Harrison McKinney to the Bank of Malone. When they got there, Mears and McKinney told Reece to remain outside with the motor running. They then drew their pistols, put on masks and burst through the doors of the bank. McKinney stood near the door, covering the tellers and customers, while Mears scooped up silver and cash. The two robbers made good their escape, picked up Dudley and headed for Chicago to party. They made the mistake, however, of leaving their driver behind with no share of the wealth for his trouble.[15]

The haul from the rural bank had been surprising, $4,052 in currency and silver according to one newspaper. Cheating their driver, however, proved to be the undoing of the robbers. Reece was quickly picked up by sheriff's officers and wasted no time in identifying Mears, Dudley and McKinney. He promised to testify against them.[16]

The three robbers were picked up in Chicago just four days after the bank job. They still had a little over $1,000 on them but the rest of the money had vanished. Indicted by the Jackson County Grand Jury, Mears, Dudley and McKinney were held in jail for a trial date of October 22nd.

As Sheriff Chambliss was trying to figure out whether Herbert Smith was really involved in the murder of Lola Cannady, the trial of the bank robbers got underway at the Jackson County Courthouse. The first day's activity consisted of drawing jurors for the case and Judge Amos Lewis set opening arguments for Wednesday, the 24th.[17]

Jury selection also was held in Marianna that day for the expected murder trial of Rudolph Godwin (alias Love Godwin). He was accused of killing Thomas Harley near Cottondale on August 13, 1934, and Deputy Dave Ham was expected to be the prosecution's key witness.[18]

Deputy Coulliette, meanwhile, spent much of the day looking into the movements of Herbert Smith at around the time of the murder of Lola Cannady. While there was no physical evidence connecting him to the crime scene, the deputy did find his movements uncertain enough to warrant taking him into custody. Despite the best efforts of the sheriff's department, however, word of Smith's possible involvement in the crime began to spread through the Malone area. To protect the suspect and allow for his continued questioning, Coulliette arrested Smith on suspicion and carried him to Marianna. From there he was immediately taken to the Leon County Jail in Tallahassee for his own safety.[19]

Despite the repeated requests from Sheriff Chambliss that he wait to take a written confession from Claude Neal if it might implicate Smith, Sheriff Gandy of Pensacola decided that it was not prudent to wait any longer to get Neal's statement in writing. The suspect was confessing freely to the murder of Lola Cannady and Gandy felt it best to record his statement for the record.

Accordingly, he took a written statement from Neal at the Escambia County (Alabama) Jail in Brewton on the night of October 22, 1934. This was the confession quoted extensively in chapter two of this narrative. It was witnessed by Sheriff G.S. Byrne and County Solicitor W.E. Brooks, both of Escambia County, Alabama. The fact that both Pensacola and Brewton are in Escambia Counties, but in different states, has led to some confusion over the years about Neal's location at the time of his statement. The actual confession, however, was given in Alabama.[20]

In his statement, Neal said that he had spent the night before Lola Cannady's murder with his common-law wife and that she was with him when he arrived at the Cannady farm on the morning of the crime. He spent some time helping Wilford Cannady (Lola's brother) "break a mule to the plow" and then left at about 12 noon and to go to the Smith house. He said that when he got there, "we went out in the field to hunt a sow." He did not

37

detail the identity of the other person or persons included in his plural "we."[21]

Claude Neal then implicated Herbert Smith in the crime, saying that as he was looking for the sow he met Herbert Smith who was already out in the field. They walked up along the north-south fence that served as the boundary between Sallie Smith's land and the Cannady farm and before long found Lola Cannady sitting by a water pump trying to clean out a hog trough. She asked Neal if he would help and Claude said that he sat down and washed out the trough for her then pumped it full of water.[22]

When Lola turned to go home, Neal said that Smith walked up, caught her by the arm, and said "How about me being with you?" Alarmed, she exclaimed, "You must be a fool!" Smith, he said, told her, "No, won't nobody know nothing about it." She told him to go on, but according to Neal, Smith then pulled her by the arm and she started calling for her brother, Wilford Cannady, who was plowing in a nearby field:

...Herbert pulled her on over the fence about four or five steps away and asked me to help him put her over the fence. Herbert choked her before he asked me to help him put her over the fence , and she stopped calling... when we got over all three of us went on down by the East and West fence to another fence running North and South and went down by the North and South fence.[23]

When they got to the corner of the woods, Neal said that Lola again resisted, saying that she did not want to go "into the woods for snakes will bite me. I am not going any farther." He claimed that Smith then forced her down on the ground and had Neal hold her by the arms while he (Herbert Smith) raped her. "She was fighting me with her hands," he said, "and trying to kick Herbert off." Neal admitted that he also raped Lola, although he claimed that "I didn't want to do that."[24]

Continuing to blame Herbert Smith for instigating the crime, he said that Smith then broke a piece from a dead oak tree and "hit her in the head with it." He said that Lola "hadn't said anything from the time we made her lie down, and she breathed a few times after Herbert hit her in the head." He said that they then dragged up two pieces of log and "laid them on her, or by the side of her. She was just breathing when we left her, she was not quite dead at that time."[25]

Neal said that he and Smith then left the scene and that he hadn't seen Smith since. He returned to his mother's house and went from there to his wife's aunt's home at Rose Lewis's place. He mentioned passing by Justice of the Peace Edgar Anderson's home and talking with him. From Anderson's place he said that he went back to his mother's, but left there again and went to Mr. John Daniel's place and was there picking peas when he was arrested.[26]

In the standard language of the time, Claude Neal then agreed that his confession was "made of my own free will and accord and without any threats, promises of reward, or hope of reward, and is entirely voluntary on my part."[27]

The confession was a mixture of fact and fiction. The physical evidence at the scene included only two sets of footprints, a man's and a woman's, not three. The trail found leading from the pump along the north-south fence to the woods also consisted of only two sets of tracks, a man's and a woman's. While he admitted to raping Lola Cannady, Neal was clearly trying to place the blame for her murder on Herbert Smith. Sheriff Chambliss, however, was not convinced. Arrangements were made to get Herbert Smith to Brewton to confront Claude Neal.

---

[1] Chambliss, Lynching Report.
[2] Mik Furie, "The Ballad of Claude Neal," The Dark Furie Blog, February 13, 2010.
[3] Speech of Sen. Mary Landrieu on the Floor of the U.S. Senate, June 13, 2005.
[4] Chambliss, Lynching Report.
[5] *Ibid.*
[6] *Ibid.*
[7] *Ibid.*
[8] *Ibid.*; *Panama City Pilot*, October 25, 1934, p. 1.
[9] Chambliss, Lynching Report.
[10] *Augusta Chronicle*, October 22, 1934, Section A, p. 3.
[11] Chambliss, Lynching Report; *Marianna Times-Courier*, October 23, 1934, p. 1.; *Panama City Pilot*, October 25, 1934, p. 1.

[12] Chambliss, Lynching Report (Note: The typed version of Sheriff Chambliss' report indicates the call from Sheriff Gandy came in at 2 a.m. The original hand-written version lists the time of the call as 9 a.m.).

[13] *Ibid.*

[14] *Ibid.*

[15] *The Miami News*, August 22, 1934; *The New York Times*, August 26, 1934.

[16] *Ibid.*

[17] *Ibid.*; Chambliss, Lynching Report.

[18] Grand Jury Indictment, State of Florida vs. Rudolph Godwin, Fall Term, 1934; Motion for Mistrial, State of Florida vs. Rudolph Godwin, October 26, 1934.

[19] Chambliss, Lynching Report; Coulliette Family Member.

[20] Chambliss, Lynching Report; "Confession of Claude Neals," October 22, 1934.

[21] "Confession of Claude Neals."

[22] *Ibid.*

[23] *Ibid.*

[24] *Ibid.*

[25] *Ibid.*

[26] *Ibid.*

[27] *Ibid.*

CHAPTER SIX

Herbert Smith is Cleared

Tuesday, October 23, 1934, was a relatively quiet day in Jackson County, the first Sheriff Flake Chambliss had enjoyed since he learned four days earlier that Lola Cannady was missing. Criminal trials continued in circuit court, but none had any connection to Claude Neal or the murder.[1]

Despite Neal's claims, Chambliss was not convinced that Herbert Smith had led the rape and murder of Lola Cannady. He had Smith moved from the Leon County Jail in Tallahassee to Escambia County Jail in Pensacola so that Sheriff Gandy could take him to confront Neal. To avoid moving Smith through Jackson County where the mob seemed to have gone quiet for a day, the sheriff had him transported via a roundabout route through Georgia and Alabama. Once in Pensacola, he was turned over to Sheriff Gandy and immediately taken to Brewton.[2]

Newspapers around the nation continued to run sensational and often inaccurate stories about the murder of Lola Cannady. They focused especially on the formation of a lynch mob in Jackson County. Some of the stories that spread across the nation included interviews obtained by local reporters with members of the Cannady family. These were often altered by editors of large newspapers, sometimes to exaggerate the already graphic content, sometimes to downplay it.

The most heartrending statement came from Lola's father, George Cannady:

...The bunch have promised me that they will give me first chance at him when they bring him back and I'll be ready. We'll put those two logs on him and ease them off by degrees. I can't get the picture of Lola out of my mind when we found her. Her throat was bruised and scratched where he had choked her so she couldn't cry out. My son was in the field about a quarter of a mile away when he saw someone talking with her at the pump, but he thought it was just one of the local boys and didn't pay much attention. He was right there in the field when she was being killed. Her head was beat in and she had been choked so hard her eyes were coming out of their sockets, her arms were broken and she was all beat up. When I get my hands on that (expletive), there isn't any telling what I'll do.[3]

One of Lola's sisters also talked with reporters. Although the writer did not identify her in the article, she was undoubtedly Hattie, the only other girl listed in the family on the 1930 census. She would have been 23 at the time of Lola's murder:

...I know there has never been anything in Jackson County that was so brutal. I'd just like to see the man who did this just once. I can't understand what the motive was for this brutal deed. To think that Claude Neal, who had been raised with my sister and me and worked for us all his life, could do such a thing – it is unbelievable. I only wish that every resident of Jackson County could view the body of my sister. If they could, they wouldn't rest until the murderer was caught and justice meted out.[4]

In the farm country around Malone, Greenwood and Bascom, the group that had organized to bring Claude Neal back definitely was not at rest. Newspapers and radio broadcasts were monitored for any information on his whereabouts and attempts were made to call in favors from friends, politicians and like-minded lawmen across the entire region. Initially, none of these sources provided any useful information. After he had been moved from Panama City to Pensacola, as far as the mob could tell, Claude Neal had vanished.

Neal remained in the Brewton jail during this time, but lawmen maintained tight secrecy over his whereabouts. Sheriff G.S. Byrne later explained to investigators in Alabama that he did everything in his power to assure Neal's security, but also expected help from Sheriff Gandy in the event of trouble:

> *When the Negro was brought to me I put him in what is known as the death cell and which is the best protected cell in the jail, and had a double lock put on the door. Sheriff Gandy advised me, however, that he would protect me and if there were any rumors of a mob being formed to take the Negro from my jail he would promptly notify me and give the necessary assistance, but as it was not to be known where the prisoner was concealed I thought there was little danger from mob violence.[5]*

Sheriff Byrne, however, does not seem to have been in direct contact with Sheriff Chambliss in Jackson County and did not have reliable information on the determination or movements of the mob. As a consequence, although he appears to have been a brave lawman determined to do his best, he and his deputies largely operated in the dark.[6]

On Wednesday morning, October 24th, the Jackson County Grand Jury convened at the courthouse in Marianna but immediately recessed for two days. State Attorney John Carter was not ready to submit the case to the grand jurors because he was waiting for word from Sheriff Gandy as to the results of the plan to have Herbert Smith confront Neal over his allegations that Smith had been involved in the murder. The trial of the three Malone bank robbers got underway, however, and continued throughout the day.[7]

In Brewton, Sheriff Gandy arrived at the Escambia County (Alabama) Jail with Herbert Smith. The confrontation did not last long. As soon as Neal saw Smith, he recanted and admitted that he had acted alone when he murdered Lola Cannady. According to Sheriff Byrne, who was present during the confrontation, Neal now confessed that he had choked and raped Lola. "I got to thinking I had done played the devil and she was half dead anyhow," he said, "So I went back and killed her."[8]

The question of why Neal would try to blame Smith for the crime remains unanswered even today. There were rumors around Jackson County that Smith had bested Neal in a fight a few days before the murder. Socialist activist Howard Kester picked up on this story when he tried to investigate the lynching of Neal for the NAACP:

...He tried to implicate another man by the name of Hubert (sic.) Smith with whom he had had a fight the Saturday previous. Both were arrested and taken to the woods and questioned. Finally Neal told the officers that he alone was guilty and they (the officers) let Smith go. Smith is now near Malone. This is straight. I got it from prime sources.[9]

The story, of course, was not straight and Kester's sources could not have been "prime" because Neal and Smith were not arrested at the same time and neither of the men was taken to the woods and questioned. The activist also mistakenly identified Herbert Smith as "Hubert" Smith. In light of such errors, it is difficult to assess the accuracy of his claim that a fight had taken place between the two men. Kester obviously did not talk to Smith, but otherwise did not identify his source.[10]

Whatever his reason for originally claiming that Smith had been the instigator of the murder, Neal recanted and cleared him when the two met face to face in the Brewton jail. Herbert Smith was taken back to Pensacola by Sheriff Gandy and held there in protective custody for his own safety. Claude Neal, meanwhile, remained in the Alabama jail and began talking freely with other inmates about the murder. When Sheriff Byrne heard this, he spoke to the prisoner and urged him to stay quiet. Bryne warned Neal that he was putting his own life at risk by talking, but the suspect replied that he knew he would "die in the electric chair and he would just as soon have a mob lynch him now so he could get his thoughts away from the electric chair."[11]

Things now began to happen very fast. Howard Kester claimed in his November 7th letter to NAACP Secretary Walter White that the mob in Jackson County was tipped to Neal's location by an unidentified person in Pensacola:

...It is known that a business man of Marianna arranged with a party in Pensacola to have word sent here the moment Neal was released from there. The word was received here and a group of men set out for Brewton immediately. Very few people with whom I have talked resent the lynching at all.[12]

This was an interesting claim, but the leaders of the mob said in the early 1980s that they actually learned of Claude Neal's location from a much more conventional source: the media. Word that Neal had confessed in Brewton leaked out and an Associated Press reporter from Mobile called Sheriff Byrne at around midnight seeking confirmation. The sheriff told the reporter that Neal had confessed, but tried to convince the journalist that the suspect was no longer in his jail.[13]

It was to no avail. The news went out over the wires and by the next morning – Thursday, October 25th – pretty much everyone in Jackson County knew where Neal was being held. The leaders of the lynch mob met to discuss the situation and quickly decided to raid the Brewton jail and see for themselves whether he was still there. The word was spread and a group of men assembled to take part in the planned assault. They were armed with pistols, shotguns and dynamite.[14]

---

[1] Chambliss, Lynching Report.

[2] *Ibid.*

[3] *Jackson County Floridan*, October 20, 1934, p. 1. (Note: The expletive in the quote was deleted by the author.).

[4] *Jackson County Floridan*, October 20, 1934, p. 1.

[5] Statement of Sheriff G.S. Byrne, Given to Hugh M. Caffey, November 1934 (hereafter Byrne Statement), Governor Miller Papers, Alabama Department of Archives and History, copy in Carswell Collection.

[6] Chambliss, Lynching Report (Note: Chambless makes no mention in his report of any contact with Byrne).

[7] *Ibid.*

[8] *Ibid.*; *Free Lance-Star*, October 27, 1934, p. 1.

[9] Howard Kester to Walter White, November 7, 1934, NAACP Papers, Part 7, Series A, Reel 9 (hereafter Kester to White, November 7, 1934).

[10] *Ibid.*

[11] Byrne Statement.

[12] Kester to White, November 7, 1934.

[13] Various newspapers carried this report.

[14] Interview with Lynch Mob Member #1.

CHAPTER SEVEN

The Shooting of Deputy Dave Ham

Thursday – October 25, 1934 – marked the real beginning of the chaos that rocked Marianna and Jackson County for days to come. It began quietly enough, with the eyes of the judicial system focused not on Claude Neal but on the Malone bank robbers.

The trial of Buford Mears, Harrison McKinney and M.F. Dudley continued in the Circuit Court of the Fourteenth Judicial Circuit. As expected, their driver Willie Reece testified against the other three, telling jurors he had been ordered by Dudley to drive Mears and McKinney to the Bank of Malone and that he had watched as they robbed the bank. Testifying on their own behalf, however, the alleged robbers claimed that they had taken only money that was owed to them. The jury was not convinced and at 4:30 p.m., all three were found guilty.[1]

In Brewton, meanwhile, Claude Neal amended his written confession by removing the references to Herbert Smith. He now claimed full responsibility for the murder of Lola Cannady, admitting both verbally and in writing that he raped and murdered her on the afternoon of October 18, 1934. Seven days had passed since the young woman's brutal slaying.[2]

As the afternoon passed, unknown to either Sheriff Chambliss in Marianna or Sheriff Byrne in Brewton, a caravan of roughly thirty cars assembled on the back roads near Malone. Most were Model A Fords, then the most common model of car in the world and one almost exclusively driven by Jackson County citizens fortunate enough to own a vehicle. Each of the cars carried three or four men, all heavily armed. Six of the men were the clear leaders of the group, some of them dressed in dark suits and others in clothing that imitated the khaki pants, plaid shirts and boots then worn by sheriff's deputies in most of the Florida Panhandle counties.[3]

The seriousness of the group was emphasized by the fact that they carried along an impressive supply of dynamite to be used in blasting the Escambia County (Alabama) Jail to pieces if that was what they had to do to get at Claude Neal. One of the men was an expert in explosives. Also accompanying the group was a man who knew Claude Neal very well. He was to identify the confessed killer so the group could be sure they had the right man. According to participants, they had no desire to "lynch an innocent man."[4]

As darkness fell, the long caravan pulled out. It avoided the main highways so that law officers along the way would not notice them and alert the sheriff in Brewton. The trip would be long and slow as the route wound its way along dirt roads and back ways across the Florida Panhandle and then into Alabama. Their departure was kept secret by the people of northeastern Jackson County and Sheriff Chambliss had no idea that an attempt to seize Neal was underway.[5]

In Marianna, meanwhile, a jury was impanelled to hear the case of Rudolph "Love" Godwin and the first witnesses were sworn. Testimony in the murder case was scheduled to begin the next morning.[6]

These procedures complete, court activity ended for the day and Sheriff Chambliss and Deputy Dave Ham moved Mears and McKinney from the holding cell into a Model A Ford to begin the trip back to the Washington County Jail in Chipley, where they were being held for their own safety. The third bank robber, M.F. Dudley, was younger than the other two and was released to go home pending his sentencing.

The black car carrying the four men made its way out of Marianna and west on U.S. Highway 90. The 1939 Works Progress Administration guide to Florida, published just five years later, described the route as "a fertile hilly area producing Satsuma oranges, pecans, sugar cane, and peanuts." Cottondale, through which the lawmen passed with their prisoners, was described by the guide in colorful terms:

COTTONDALE...is a farming, fishing and hunting center. The fish in neighboring streams and lakes are so voracious, it is said, that fisherman have to stand out of sight behind trees while baiting their hooks. Unlike visitors, old residents refuse to fish on Sundays, for, as one explained, 'I ain't got nothing' else to do on weekdays.'[7]

The four men may even have talked about the things they had in common, hunting, fishing and farming, as they made their way along the winding highway. Chambliss and Ham may have discussed the Claude Neal case. Whatever their topic of conversation, they did not reach Chipley.

As the Model A passed through the pine woods and fields between Cottondale and Chipley, Buford Mears suddenly pulled a pistol and opened fire. Deputy Ham drew his own pistol and returned fire as the car careened off the road. By the time Sheriff Chambliss could knock the gun from Mears' hand and subdue him, both Ham and the other bank robber, Harrison McKinney, had been seriously wounded. [8]

In a motion filed in circuit court the next morning, State Attorney John Carter provided more information on the wounding of the deputy:

...Dave Ham, while transporting certain prisoners from Marianna to the County Jail at Chipley, Florida., at about 8:00 P.M. last night, was seriously wounded by being shot with a pistol by one of said prisoners. Said pistol was a 32 caliber, and the bullet entered said Dave Ham in the left arm, passing through his left arm and into the left side of his body just below the shoulder, and passed through his body just below the right shoulder. That he is now confined in the hospital of Dr. Watson, in Chipley, Florida, and is in a serious condition as a result of said wound....[9]

The wounded prisoner, McKinney, was brought back to Marianna to the Baltzell Hospital while Ham, as noted above, was taken to Chipley for care. The shooting of a law enforcement officer always creates chaos and this incident was no different. Besides worrying about his wounded employee and a wounded prisoner as well, Sheriff Chambliss had to get Buford Mears to a secure location while also trying to find out how he had managed to get his hands on a pistol.

That information soon came out and deputies arrested Horace Johns on charges that he had slipped Mears the gun during the trial. The bank robber had managed to keep it concealed until he pulled it out and started shooting inside the sheriff's car.[10]

While the sheriff and his deputies tried to deal with this situation, the caravan of cars driven by the lynch mob slowly made its way along the back roads along the line dividing Florida from Alabama. When Mears opened fire that evening, he created such chaos that Chambliss was unable to give due attention to the situation in the northeastern part of the county. In fact, the sheriff spent much of the night dealing with the chaos caused by the failed escape attempt and in worrying about his severely wounded deputy.

Events now began to take on a life of their own. With the sheriff in Chipley waiting to learn the results of the surgery on Ham and the people of Marianna electrified by news of the shooting, the lynch mob slowly closed in on Brewton, Alabama. They had picked their route well and avoided all contact with law enforcement as they moved west. When they reached their destination later that night, their arrival would come as a total surprise.

The gunfire between Cottondale and Chipley on the evening of October 25th played a significant but often underestimated or even ignored role in the events of the next two days. The attention of the sheriff and his deputies was necessarily distracted at a critical moment.

The calmness that he likely felt was finally settling on the county was shattered when Buford Mears pulled a .32 caliber pistol and shot Deputy Dave Ham. The evening of the 25th turned chaotic and the chaos would continue for days to come. Literally before the sheriff had time to even consider what was happening, events began to overwhelm him.

---

[1] Chambliss, Lynching Report; Records of Mears, McKinney and Dudley Trial, Jackson County Courthouse, Marianna, Florida.

[2] Chambliss, Lynching Report.

[3] Byrne Statement; Interviews with Lynch Mob Members #1 and #2.

[4] *Ibid.*; Hatcher Interview.

[5] *Ibid.*

[6] Chambliss, Lynching Report.

[7] Federal Writers' Project of the Works Projects Administration for the State of Florida, *Florida: A Guide to the Southernmost State*, Oxford University Press, 1939, p. 444.

[8] Chambliss, Lynching Report; *St. Petersburg Times*, October 28, 1934, p. 3.

[9] Motion for Mistrial in State of Florida vs. Rudolph Godwin, alias Love Godwin, submitted by State Attorney John Carter, Jr., October 26, 1934.

[10] *St. Petersburg Times*, October 28, 1934.

CHAPTER EIGHT

The Kidnapping of Claude Neal

The first episode in the lynch mob's raid on the Escambia County (Alabama) Jail may have taken place on the afternoon of October 25, 1934, even before the attempted escape of the Malone bank robbers. An account of the rather bizarre episode was given to an investigator in Alabama in early November, but the reliability of the story is not clear. It did not come from Sheriff Byrne or from any of his deputies.

According to the story, a man came into the courthouse and brought up the subject of Claude Neal with two local residents. He claimed to live on the outskirts of Brewton, but no one recognized him. He said he had heard that a mob of 300 to 400 people had organized in Florida and had found out that Neal was being held in the Brewton jail. He went on to mention that he thought Sheriff Byrne had received instructions to send the suspect to Pensacola.[1]

The statement was considered reliable by historian James R. McGovern who included it in *Anatomy of a Lynching*. There are, however, serious problems with the claim. The mysterious stranger - McGovern seems to insinuate he was a scout of some type for the Jackson County group - supposedly told the people he approached in Brewton that news of Neal's presence in the jail there had been carried back to Jackson County by

Herbert Smith who had been released in Florida. On the afternoon of October 25th, however, Smith was still being held in protective custody at the jail in Pensacola.[2]

The fact that Smith had not yet returned to Jackson County is a major flaw in the reliability of the story. Another flaw in the tale is that the source was not the sheriff himself, even though he was quite thorough in his subsequent statement of what happened in Brewton that night. The story was never picked up by the media of the day and, when interviewed in 1982, none of the surviving lynch mob members knew anything about such a scout or spy being sent to Brewton ahead of their main caravan.[3]

About the best that can be said about the tale is that it was told during the investigation ordered by Governor Miller of Alabama, but not by the sheriff, jailor or any employee of the sheriff's office or police force in Brewton. It included detail that was not accurate and may have been one of the many rumors that surfaced in the weeks after the Claude Neal lynching

The real lynch mob reached the outskirts of Brewton shortly before 1 o'clock on the morning of Friday, October 26, 1934. They halted in a rural area from which they could see the lights of the community and smoked hand-rolled cigarettes while they again discussed their plan.[4]

The men had learned from their previous efforts to find Neal. After having moved in large force against the jails in Chipley and Panama City and being eluded by officers in those towns, they now implemented a much different strategy. Instead of rolling immediately into Brewton, the men split up and positioned groups of three or four cars to watch and if necessary block the roads leading into and out of town. A group of three cars then rolled into Brewton to scout the situation and learn the layout of the town. This, of course, would have been unnecessary had the "stranger" supposedly seen in Brewton earlier in the day actually been a member of their group. A final group of three cars held back on the edge of town to await developments.[5]

The first men to enter Brewton spent some time driving the streets and getting the feel of the town. Local police saw them checking out the Escambia County Courthouse and stopped to talk, but the men identified themselves as law officers from Florida and said they needed to see the sheriff. Because two of the strangers were wearing dark suits and the third was dressed like a Florida deputy in khaki pants, plaid flannel shirt and boots, their story seemed reasonable. The Brewton officer told them that

Sheriff Byrne was at home, but gave them directions to the jail. The local policeman obviously knew that Claude Neal was being there, but clearly had not heard any rumors that a mob was on its way to Brewton or he likely would have been more circumspect.[6]

At around 1:45 a.m. three cars pulled into the Gulf Station near the intersection of the roads to Andalusia (U.S. 29) and Milton (Florida Street). Station attendant T.J. Criggers was awakened and two of the drivers had him fill up their vehicles. He noticed that the two cars he gassed up had Florida tags but since he did not fill up the third he didn't notice where it was from. The men, he said, were "just the ordinary run of people" and he thought there were probably five in each vehicle. He only described the dress of four of them, recalling one was wearing a blue suit but that the other three were dressed in overalls.[7]

The men asked Criggers which county they were in and the name of the local sheriff, but he didn't seem to find this strange. Likely this was because he was tired and just wanted to go back to bed, which he did as soon as they left the station. He did recall that they came in from the direction of Andalusia and asked how far they were from Florida.[8]

Oddly, one of the two men who later claimed they talked with the mysterious "stranger" at the courthouse was the next person to report seeing the lynch mob members as they moved around Brewton. Dan Brantley had driven into town because his daughter worked at a textile mill there and her shift change was coming up at 2 a.m. Brantley passed the Gulf station in East Brewton at around 1:45 a.m. and noticed that three cars were parked there with 15 or so men milling around. He immediately assumed they were the rumored lynch mob (which neither the sheriff nor city police knew about).[9]

The surveillance mission carried out in Brewton had achieved its goal of locating the jail and finding out if the sheriff was up and about that night. The two parties that planned to carry out the actual raid now met and finalized their plan. This done, the first group of three cars turned and drove back across the Murder Creek Bridge into town. It was now around 2 a.m.[10]

As the men from Jackson County held their final meeting on the outskirts of town, Dan Brantley spotted a Brewton police car and passed along a warning that he had seen men at the Gulf station and thought they might be part of a lynch mob of 300 people he had heard were on their way to take Claude Neal. Officer R.A. Strong immediately warned Jailer Jake Shanholtzer of the possible threat.[11]

The news took Shanholtzer by surprise. Alone in the jail at the time, he immediately called Sheriff Byrne and asked for help. Byrne, who lived just a short distance away, jumped in his car and rushed to the jail:

When I got to the jail there were two or three cars there and two of the men got out of one of the cars and talked to me and one got out holding an automatic shotgun on me. They demanded the Negro of me and I gave them the assurance that he was not in the jail, but had been carried away. I attempted to placate them by assuring them that if he was in my jail I would be glad to turn him over to them, and went so far as to offer carrying them through the jail and letting them see for themselves, feeling that I had safely concealed the Negro in the death cell, and that after looking over the Negro prisoners in the regular cells, they should leave satisfied. They expressed confidence that I had told them the truth, shook hands with me and left.[12]

Byrne's description of the demeanor of the men was consistent with reports of their earlier meeting with Sheriff Hobbs in Panama City, Florida. They were polite but firm. The one difference this time was that one displayed a weapon, whereas none had been shown during their appearance in Panama City.

The sheriff indicated that two of the men were well dressed in dark clothes, probably a reference to suits similar to the blue suit described by the gas station attendant. The third, he said, was wearing "khaki clothes."[13]

After waiting a few minutes for a deputy to reach the jail, Sheriff Byrne got back in his car and started to follow the route taken by the men. He slowly tailed them until he reached the bridge over Murder Creek and could tell that they were continuing down the road to Milton, Florida (Florida Street).[14]

Now realizing that there was a very real threat to Neal's safety, the sheriff turned around and drove back into town already making plans to move the prisoner to Evergreen, Alabama, as soon as possible. As Byrne approached Brewton City Hall, he noticed two city police officers standing there and stopped to fill them in on the situation and tell them that he might need their help.[15]

What neither Byrne nor the city officers knew, however, was that the first approach to the jail by members of the lynch mob had been a feint, intended to draw away the sheriff or any other officers they might encounter there. The strategy worked perfectly. After reassuring the jailer that everything would be ok, the deputy called in by the sheriff left in his own car to follow Byrne in case he needed back up. Almost as soon as he left, a second group of three cars pulled up to the jail.[16]

A group of between 12 and 15 armed men piled out of these cars and stormed through the outer doors of the jail, taking jailer Jake Shanholtzer by surprise. The first men through the door aimed pistols at Shanholtzer and demanded the keys to the cells where black prisoners were held. Even more alarming than the men with guns was a man the jailer saw come through the door behind them. His arms were filled with sticks of dynamite:

... He said that he would blow the place off the corner if they did not find what they were looking for. They took the keys from me and being unable to unlock the cell, held their guns on a white trusty in the jail and compelled him to unlock the doors. They might have overlooked the Negro in the death cell if he had not rushed to the door to see what it was all about, but as soon as they saw him they expressed satisfaction, had the cell unlocked and took him away.[17]

As soon as they took Neal from the extra-secure "death cell," the men tied his hands behind him with a plow line (a piece of rope used by farmers to guide a mule or horse when plowing). Shanholtzer heard one of them tell Claude that he did not have long to live and that if he needed to talk to the Lord, he had better do it then. They also told Shanholtzer: "We're going to take him to Marianna, Fla., and turn him over to the girl's father and let him do what he wants to with him."[18]

The raid on the Brewton Jail took place at some point between 2 and 3 a.m. and was over quickly. Claude Neal was placed in the back seat of a black Model A Ford and armed men climbed in on each side of him. The car carrying the prisoner led the way out of town, followed by the other two vehicles. The Florida men picked up speed as they passed Sheriff Byrne and the two Brewton police officers talking in front of the city hall. They were quickly across the Murder Creek Bridge and on their way down the road to Milton, Florida. They crossed the Florida line a short time later at the community of Dixonville.[19]

Stunned by the sight of the cars speeding past him, the sheriff rushed back up the street to the jail and found that he had been decoyed and Neal was gone. Realizing that the men would be approaching the Florida line even then (it was only 8 miles south of Brewton), Byrne immediately got on the phone and woke up Sheriff Gandy in Pensacola to let him know that the suspect was in the hands of the lynch mob.[20]

[1] Statements of Lum Jeter and Dan Brantley taken by Hugh M. Caffey, November 1934, Governor Miller Papers, Alabama Department of Archives and History (Copy from E.W. Carswell Collection).

[2] James R. McGovern, *Anatomy of a Lynching*, pp. 60-63.

[3] Interviews with Lynch Mob Members #1 and #2.

[4] *Ibid.*

[5] *Ibid.*

[6] Statement of Officer R.A. Strong, Brewton Police Department, taken by Hugh M. Caffey, November 1934, Governor Miller Papers, Alabama Department of Archives and History (Copy from E.W. Carswell Collection).

[7] Statement of T.J. Criggers taken by Hugh M. Caffey, November 1934, Governor Miller Papers, Alabama Department of Archives and History (Copy from E.W. Carswell Collection).

[8] *Ibid.*

[9] Statement of Dan Brantley taken by Hugh M. Caffey, November 1934, Governor Miller Papers, Alabama Department of Archives and History (Copy from E.W. Carswell Collection).

[10] Interviews with Lynch Mob Members #1 and #2.

[11] Statements of Dan Brantley and Officer R.A. Strong, taken by Hugh M. Caffey, November 1934, Governor Miller Papers, Alabama Department of Archives and History (Copies from E.W. Carswell Collection).

[12] Statement of Sheriff G.S. Byrne taken by Hugh M. Caffey, November 1934, Governor Miller Papers, Alabama Department of Archives and History (Copy from E.W. Carswell Collection).

[13] *Ibid.*

[14] *Ibid.*

[15] *Ibid.*

[16] *Ibid.*

[17] Statement of Jake Shanholtzer taken by Hugh M. Caffey, November 1934, Governor Miller Papers, Alabama Department of Archives and History (Copy from E.W. Carswell Collection).

[18] *Ibid.*; *Seattle Daily Times*, October 26, 1934, p. 4 (Shanholtzer's statement also was widely quoted in other newspapers of the day).
[19] Statement of Jake Shanholtzer; Interviews with Lynch Mob Members #1 and #2.
[20] Statement of Sheriff G.S. Byrne.

CHAPTER NINE

Prelude to a Lynching

Author's Note: This chapter and the two that follow it are based in part on interviews conducted more than twenty years ago with two members of the "Committee of Six" that lynched Claude Neal. They are no longer living nor are any of the other men in their group. Their names are being withheld from publication as a courtesy to their families.

The small group of cars carrying Claude Neal and his kidnappers reached Jackson County at around 9 a.m. on Friday, October 26, 1934. They arrived first in Campbellton where they learned the latest information on what had happened in the county since their departure, including the somewhat distorted details of the attempted escape of the bank robbers and the shooting of Deputy Ham. Tired from the stress and difficulty of their journey and angry from their conversations with Neal, the news steeled in their minds that crime was out of control in Jackson County and that something had to be done to send a message.

The drive from Brewton back to Jackson County had taken roughly six hours, largely because the men had avoided the main roads and populated areas hoping to elude any pursuit. They need not have worried. Once they got across the Florida line and out of the jurisdiction of Sheriff Byrne, there was no coordinated effort to catch them.

The same drive today, using the preferred route, would take less than two and one-half hours. In 1934, though, using the poorly maintained back roads and driving Model A Fords, it was a daunting journey. By the time the men reached Campbellton, they had driven more than 10 hours, raided a jail, kidnapped a murder suspect and eluded pursuit, all with very little sleep and very little food.

At Campbellton the men stopped and discussed their plan. One of the cars in the three car group was sent on to the Cannady farm to inform George Cannady that Neal was back in Jackson County. The agreed upon message was that they would deliver their prisoner to the Cannady house that night between 8 and 9 p.m. Lola's father would be given the first opportunity to do harm to the man they firmly believed had killed his daughter.

The other two cars, carrying six men and Claude Neal, gassed up and headed east through the farm country between Greenwood and Malone. They continued to avoid the main roads and in about one hour passed through the fading community of Parramore in eastern Jackson County. Once a thriving riverboat town, the village was in a decline brought on by both the Great Depression and the slow end of paddlewheel riverboat traffic on the Chattahoochee River.

The men, who would be known thereafter as the "Committee of Six," knew the Parramore area well and had in mind a good hiding place in the edge of the swamps near the river. Called Peri (pronounced "pea-rye") Landing, the spot had been an important riverboat stop for many years. Cotton, timber, bales of cotton and even gopher tortoises and boxes of catfish had once been loaded onto steamboats there for transport either up the river to Fort Gaines, Eufaula and Columbus or downstream to Chattahoochee and Apalachicola. At its height, a number of such landings had served the Parramore area, but by 1934 only nearby Parramore Landing remained in use. Peri and other landings like it had been abandoned and were slowly being reclaimed by the swamp.[1]

They did not go all the way down to the landing, but instead stopped at a point just in the edge of the woods where the road passed down a deep cut as the land sloped down into the river bottom. The spot was isolated, with the nearest house more than one mile away. A wide field opened just a few yards away, allowing the men to see anyone that might approach via the most likely route. Only the men in the car sent to the Cannady house knew where they had gone. Otherwise, their destination was a closely guarded secret.

The men pulled their cars off into the woods and picked a spot by the road cut. Claude Neal was chained to an oak tree with trace chains (normally used to connect plows to horses or mules), the men lit a fire and everyone settled in to wait for nightfall and the planned lynching.

In Marianna, just one hour before the men holding Neal reached Jackson County, Sheriff Chambliss arrived at the courthouse after a long and sleepless night. In just the last twelve hours, he had been involved in a shootout, automobile accident and investigation of a bloody escape attempt. One of his four deputies lay near death in a Chipley hospital, while one of the bank robbers was slowly dying at the Baltzell Hospital in Marianna. He walked into his office to find Sheriff Gandy of Pensacola on the phone, relaying the news that Claude Neal had been taken from the jail in Brewton during the night by a group of armed men. Their destination, Gandy said, was unknown other than that they had headed for Milton, Florida. The Pensacola sheriff told Chambliss that he did not know if Neal was still alive.[2]

A murder trial was set to convene in circuit court that morning. Rudolph Godwin, also known as Love Godwin, was accused of shooting Thomas Harley near Cottondale. The prosecution's key witness, however, was Deputy Dave Ham.

Ham had tracked down Godwin following the crime, but was mortally wounded and would not live out the next 48 hours. Without his principal witness, State Attorney John Carter had no choice but to request a mistrial:

The State would respectfully show that after the said Dave Ham was duly sworn as a witness... and after the Court had adjourned until this morning, the said Dave Ham, while transporting certain prisoners from Marianna to the County Jail at Chipley, Florida, at about 8:00 P.M. last night, was seriously wounded by being shot with a pistol by one of said prisoners... That he is now confined in the hospital of Dr. Watson, in Chipley, Florida, and is in a serious condition as a result of said wound, and utterly unable to attend Court at this time and will be utterly unable to attend Court for at least two weeks. That the inability of said witness to be present for this trial is due to no fault of the plaintiff, and if the State is required to proceed with the trial at this time, or at any time prior to the time said witness is able to attend Court as a witness for the State a serious miscarriage of justice will result.[3]

The motion was sworn to before Circuit Court Clerk H. Anderson Bowles, the same local leader that had taken to the bed of a pickup truck a few days earlier in an unsuccessful effort to talk the angry citizens out of trying to lynch Claude Neal. It was granted.[4]

With the murder trial no longer an issue, the exhausted sheriff and his equally tired deputies focused on continuing their investigation of the violent escape attempt and the whereabouts of Claude Neal. The sheriff himself returned to Chipley to check on the condition of Deputy Ham and to further interview Buford Mears. An additional suspect in the bloody escape attempt was taken into custody that morning. Horace Johns, the man believed responsible for slipping Mears the .32 caliber pistol he used in the attack was brought to the county jail in Marianna.

Contrary to widespread modern speculation and innuendo, the sheriff and his officers did not forget or ignore the danger facing Claude Neal. "Ways and means of saving Neal from mob discussed and considered," he noted in his report to Governor Dave Sholtz, "but whereabouts and destination of mob not known."[5]

The latter statement has been ridiculed by many modern writers based on the erroneous belief that the lynching was advertised in newspapers and on the radio and was attended by thousands of people. This was simply not the case.

A thorough review of the newspapers and logbooks of the radio stations that served the area in 1934 reveals that not a single advertisement promoting the lynching was run. In fact, most papers were prevented by their deadlines from even reporting that Neal had been taken from the Brewton jail until after he was actually dead. The claim that ads were published or aired inviting white citizens to attend Neal's killing is patently false and one of the more blatant examples of a widely believed but completely untrue statement about the lynching. All the sheriff was able to learn about Neal was that he was being held in a remote area. He did not even know whether he was in Florida or Alabama. The Committee of Six had picked their spot well and their secrecy was complete.

At the Cannady farm, meanwhile, anticipation was growing for what was expected to be a public or spectacle lynching. The news that Claude Neal had been brought back to Jackson County and would be turned over to George Cannady that night between 8 and 9 p.m. was spread by word of mouth. There were very few telephones in northeastern Jackson County in 1934. No radio or newspaper ads were run. People simply heard about the planned lynching and passed the news on to their friends, neighbors and relatives.

Some area afternoon newspapers, including the *Dothan Eagle,* came out with the news that Neal had been taken from Brewton. An *Eagle* reporter called the Jackson County sheriff's office for comment, but was told that officers did not know where Neal was being held and had received no news of a planned public lynching. This was true. While Chambliss and his men could speculate as to the intent of the men holding the prisoner, the gunfight of the previous night had staggered them at a critical moment. Not only where they overwhelmed by the violence of the event, they were actively searching for additional suspects while dealing with the critical wounding of both a deputy and a prisoner. [6]

Sheriff Chambliss that afternoon declined an offer from a member of the governor's staff to deploy National Guard troops to Jackson County. He later faced much criticism for this decision, but at the time he declined the offer of help he legitimately did not see a need for the troops. No one knew where Claude Neal was being held and the investigation of the attempted escape by the bank robbers was under control. The situation in Marianna was peaceful and there was no evidence of the violence to come. In short, Chambliss was being honest when he told the governor's office that he saw no need for troops in Jackson County.

The *Jackson County Floridan* of that day came out before news reached Jackson County of the taking of Neal by the mob. It included no reference to a planned lynching and no reference to his location, although there was breaking news regarding his confession:

The Jackson County Floridan was advised last night from official sources that Claud Neal, held for murder in the death of Miss Lola Cannidy (sic.), has made a complete confession to the crime and intends to plead guilty when arraigned. No one else is implicated in the crime, and his confession does not implicate any other person. [7]

The paper also, it is worth noting, published a sadly premature commendation to Sheriff Chambliss and his officers for the job they had done preventing a lynching:

Although many have strongly favored the court of Judge Lynch for the brutal slayer of a Jackson County girl this week, local officers have spared no effort to uphold their oath of office and protect their prisoner. In many instances this action has been contrary to the wishes of citizens, but the concensus of opinion is that one crime in a week is enough.[8]

John Winslett, then affiliated with the *Floridan*, wrote much of its coverage of events surrounding the Claude Neal lynching. He indicated in 1984 that while there had been rumor and talk on the streets that "someone" might lynch Neal, no one in Marianna really thought it possible. The sheriff had gotten the suspect out of the county before the country men came in looking for him and talk had calmed considerably by the afternoon of the 26th. Well connected to Sheriff Chambliss and several of his officers, Winslett learned from them that a mob had taken Neal from Brewton but also learned that the lawmen had no idea where he was being held or if he was still alive.[9]

He recalled that Marianna was not alive with speculation about a possible lynching that day, but that people instead were excited about the anticipated arrival of the so-called "Chevrolet Caravan." This parade of seventy-five new Chevrolet cars was making its way north through Florida from the recently concluded American Legion convention in Miami. After a morning stop at Silver Springs, the cars and the Legionnaires packed into them were expected to reach Marianna on Sunday.[10]

The Chipola Hotel was booked solid and red, white and blue bunting and flags adorned the city:

The motorcade will be under supervision of Fred Emich, Chicago Chevrolet dealer and commander of Chipilly post. The bodies of the cars will be painted dark blue and the wheels golden to correspond with the Legion colors, while the Legion insignia will be painted on the sides. The motorcade will be entertained by Chevrolet dealers and Legion posts en route and will number 75 passenger cars and five trucks for carrying baggage and band instruments... The caravan will arrive in Marianna at 9 a.m. on Sunday, October 28th.[11]

In addition to Legionnaires passing through Marianna on their way home, the city was also alive with people arriving for a Young Democrats meeting. Hundreds of delegates from across the Third Congressional District began showing up in Marianna on Friday, eagerly anticipating a downtown speech by noted Florida politician Claude Pepper:

Hon. Claude Pepper of Tallahassee, one of Florida's outstanding democratic orators, will speak at two o'clock from the band stand in the plaza on the subject of 'Proposed Constitutional Amendments," which are to be voted on in the election November 6. The morning session will be followed by a luncheon at Hotel Chipola, which will be the Convention Headquarters.[12]

In fact, while the newspaper made no mention of a planned lynching at the Cannady farm, it did encourage people to gather the next day in downtown Marianna to hear Pepper's speech:

The purpose of the meeting here is to bring the young democrats of the district together for discussion of matters vital to the party, and to enlarge the various county organizations. All young democrats, whether members of the county organization or not, are strongly urged to be present at the Grammar school auditorium, when the sessions open at ten o'clock, and to participate in every feature of the assembly. It is hoped also that a large crowd will greet Claude Pepper when he speaks from the bandstand at two o'clock.[13]

A protest by members of the Jackson County Purification League was also set to take place in Marianna that Saturday. It has been claimed by several modern writers – including one distinguished university professor – that the Purification League was a racist organization with the primary objective of removing all blacks from government relief rolls during the darkest days of the Great Depression. Not only is the assertion completely false, but it is outright slander against the efforts of organization leader Wankard Pooser.

When Pooser and his followers used the term "purification," they were not talking about race but instead their determination to see the relief system purified of waste, graft and corruption so that more money reached the pockets of the most impoverished Americans. In a letter to the editor of the *Jackson County Floridan* published on the day of the Claude Neal lynching, for example, Pooser made not one mention of race, but instead railed against the money being absorbed by highly-paid administrators and officials in the Federal Emergency Relief Agency (FERA). These same people, he said, were 1,500% more selfish than the average American and he was infuriated by their requirement that destitute Jackson County citizens were being required to "drive, walk or crawl" ten to twenty miles from their homes into Marianna to receive their small relief payments.[14]

A vocal opponent of a plan to spend the majority of the county's FERA education improvement dollars at Marianna High School to the detriment of rural schools, Pooser also made tongue in cheek reference to recent newspaper reports praising the accomplishments of the local business community:

> *Our League stands ready at all times to co-operate with the FERA, the Chamber of Commerce and the Marianna Merchants Association, (which, judging from last week's report of the Chamber, are all one), in any plans which will result in a maximum of relief, equitably distributed, with a minimum of administrative expense, but the Jackson County Purification League will fight 'till Gabrael blows his trumpet against the selfish and unfair practices that now prevail.*[15]

Much like participants in modern protest movements, Purification League members made their points with banners, marches, parades and skits. They even produced a one-act drama called "Robber's Roost.–A Parody." A comedic production that targeted FERA and its managers, plans for the drama were announced with typical Pooser flourish: "The hungry and destitute should attend this by all means and learn what becomes of a sizable portion of the funds allotted for their relief, and how relief is mis-administered in Jackson County."[16]

So little was trouble expected in Marianna that weekend that community leaders planned a band concert Friday night at the Plaza downtown. Citizens and visitors alike were encouraged to come out and enjoy free music under the stars.[17]

Prelude to a Lynching

About twelve miles to the north, however, a scene was developing that would destroy all of the hopes building in the hearts and minds of Marianna's business and civic leaders that crystal clear Friday afternoon. People started showing up at the Cannady farm.

---

[1] For a detailed history of the Parramore area, please see *Old Parramore: The History of a Florida Ghost Town* by this author (available in both Kindle and print editions).
[2] Chambliss, Lynching Report.
[3] Motion for Mistrial, State of Florida vs. Rudolph Godwin, Alisas Love Godwin, October 26, 1934, Circuit Court Records, Jackson County Courthouse.

[4] *Ibid.*
[5] Chambliss, Lynching Report.
[6] *Dothan Eagle*, October 26, 1934, p. 1.
[7] *Jackson County Floridan*, October 26, 1934, p. 1.
[8] *Ibid.*
[9] Interview with John Winslett, September 12, 1984.
[10] *Ibid.*
[11] *Jackson County Floridan,* October 26, 1934, p. 3 (Note: The spelling "Chipilly" in the article is correct and does not refer to nearby Chipley, Florida).
[12] *Ibid.*
[13] *Ibid.*
[14] *Ibid.*
[15] *Ibid.*
[16] *Ibid.*
[17] *Ibid.*

CHAPTER TEN

Chaos at the Cannady Farm

The fields around the Cannady house had grown quiet during the week as the excitement diminished and people returned to their homes and crops. This changed on the morning of Friday, October 26th, when the car carrying some of the men from the Brewton raid arrived with news that Claude Neal was in their hands.

As the members of the Cannady family started telling their relatives and neighbors, word that a lynching would take place at the farm between 8 and 9 p.m. began to ripple through the area like lightning. A correspondent for the *Dothan Eagle* picked up on the news in time to get a report into the afternoon edition of the paper:

> *As disclosed by an informant in touch with the mob, the Negro is to be carried to the spot where he committed the crime a week ago, mutilated and tied to the stake. There, the men folks of the dead girl are to have the first blow – and then, The Eagle's informant said, the Negro will be mutilated and burned at the stake.*
>
> *This will take place just after dark and crown the week's hunt for the Negro which has carried determined mobsmen into every county seat in*

Northwest Florida and culminated with the assault on the Brewton jail where the jailer was cowed by guns and the Negro removed.[1]

At around noon, a trickle of people began returning to the farm. This trickle became a stream and eventually a river as the afternoon went on, especially after the *Dothan Eagle* came out, alerting residents of the nearby areas of Southeast Alabama and Southwest Georgia that Neal had been taken from the Brewton jail and that the Cannady family expected to kill him that night. The paper mentioned that white people were being invited to the lynching, but – as was noted in the last chapter – ran no ads encouraging attendance.

Things were initially calm and peaceful at the farm. The crowd gathered in the field by the hog pen where Lola was killed and people spent most of the afternoon talking or speculating about what would happen when Neal was produced that night. Probably the most accurate account of the situation was provided by the *Marianna Times-Courier*, the only newspaper with a correspondent actually on the scene. Although some reporters would later claim that the crowd at the farm numbered 8,000 or 9,000, the *Times-Courier* estimated that the actual number was around 3,000. The people were described as "well organized" by the paper, which noted that "men, women and children awaited in 'ringside' seats in the field."[2]

Other papers, basing their reports on second-hand information or outright fabrication, made a variety of claims about the crowd. Humorous speeches were said to have been given and one report even claimed that the Committee of Six appeared before the mob, despite the fact that all six of its members remained hidden in the woods at Peri Landing that afternoon and evening.

The NAACP repeated some of these accounts in its published report on the lynching:

Men, women and children were numbered in the vast throng that came to witness the lynching. It is reported from reliable sources that the little children, some of them mere tots, who lived in the Greenwood neighborhood, waited with sharpened sticks for the return of Neal's body.[3]

Residents of Jackson County have long maintained, however, that the "tots" from around Greenwood were not on the scene and that most of the people there actually had come down from Alabama and Georgia. Modern writers usually smirk at such claims, but basic research in the local newspapers reveals that the citizens of both Malone and Greenwood were present in their own towns that Friday night.

October 26th marked the beginning of the Halloween weekend and hundreds of local people actually turned out with their children to attend Halloween carnivals in both Greenwood and Malone. These events, according to the *Jackson County Floridan*, lasted for hours. People simply could not have been in two places at once:

The outstanding event in the social life of Greenwood the past week was the Hallowe'en Carnival held at the school building last Friday night. There were four hours filled with hilarity; there was first the plate lunch to put you in the proper mood, and after that all kinds of hallowe'en games; booths where for a nickel you could see the wonders of nature, know the past, present and future or look on mysteries that would make your hair stand on end. There were prizes for the best costumes, and Prof. Allison as Daniel Boone, (just down from the mountains) was unanimously conceded the best, although Mrs. Allison as Aunt Jemima ran a close second.[4]

The purpose of the carnival, besides providing entertainment for area families, was to raise money. The chairperson, Miss Francis Olive, reported a total profit of $67.63. While this is a small sum by today's standards, it was an impressive result for a community carnival during the days of the Great Depression. Farm laborers around Greenwood often worked from sun up until sundown for 25 cents. The collection of so much hard-earned money by the organizers of the carnival is an indication that it was well-attended.[5]

A similar event also took place in Malone the same evening and it is worth noting that both carnivals were hailed as successes by their organizers. The presence of so many people enjoying family entertainment in the two towns is a significant indication that most local families stayed away from the gathering at the Cannady farm. There were undoubtedly local people in the crowd there and children were certainly present, but local eyewitnesses were probably correct in their assertions that many of the people in the crowd had come from outside the area.[6]

This is logical considering the close association of the Malone, Greenwood and Bascom area with Alabama and Georgia. The railroad, as has been noted, linked Malone and Greenwood with Dothan, but did not extend on into Marianna. The peanut mills in Malone, in fact, had been established by Alabama interests. Greenwood, like Malone, depended heavily on the railroad as transportation for its peanuts and cotton harvested from surrounding farms. It was natural then that the two towns developed a strong relationship with Dothan as they were part of its sphere of economic influence.

When the *Dothan Eagle* had published a front page story on Friday reporting that a lynching was expected at the Cannady place that night, some people from the paper's circulation area decided to drift down to Florida and check out the scene. Local eyewitnesses later claimed that this led to a pretty steady flow of traffic from Southeast Alabama and Southwest Georgia to the farm that afternoon.[7]

Additional support for local claims about the makeup of the crowd at the Cannady farm was provided inadvertently by the NAACP. The organization sent a Socialist Party politician and labor organizer named Howard Kester to Marianna after the lynching on a mission to obtain as many of the "gruesome facts" as possible. He subsequently reported that people from as many as eight states were on hand at the Cannady place in hopes of viewing the lynching. Most of Kester's information was second-hand, but this claim was widely repeated in newspapers of the time. Whether he was the source of those claims or the papers were actually his sources is not clear.[8]

If people from eight states were on hand at the Cannady farm, it is reasonable that quite a few of the men in the crowd were Legionnaires on their way home from the Miami convention. The farm was just off both the railroad and the main road that led north from Greenwood and Malone to Dothan. A second road passed not far to the east, linking Greenwood, Bascom and Neal's Landing with the town of Donalsonville, Georgia. Eyewitnesses said that cars lined both sides of the roads leading to the Cannady farm, so it would have been easy for anyone passing by to see that something major was taking place.[9]

The crowd grew to its largest point just before nightfall, as the rumored time for the lynching neared. No one knew exactly what was going to happen, but several men did speak to crowd members urging calmness. The Cannady family members remained in the house, waiting for the Committee of Six to bring Claude Neal to them to answer for the rape and murder. They had no doubts as to his guilt.

The sheer size of the crowd, however, alarmed the men that had gone to Brewton and brought Neal back. Many of the people were armed and there was legitimate fear that gunfire might break out when Neal was brought to the scene. With so many onlookers present, the risk of additional people being hurt was extremely high. Unsure of what to do, the men loosely coordinating the event sent a messenger to their leaders in the Committee of Six. These deliberations caused a delay in events. 8 p.m. came and went, but there was no sign of the black cars, the Committee of Six or Claude Neal.

The messenger, meanwhile, reached Peri Landing to discuss the situation with the men waiting there. Claude Neal was still chained to an oak tree, but had not been physically harmed. It was now dark in the swamp and the men gathered around their fire and debated what they should do. They had planned all along to deliver their prisoner to George Cannady, but the fear that people in the crowd might be hurt alarmed them. After a brief discussion it was decided that the messenger should go back to the farm and a spokesman there should explain their concern and ask some of the people to leave. When the size of the crowd had dwindled to the point that it was thought safe, they would produce Neal and move forward with the lynching.

The messenger returned and the crowd, which by now was losing its patience with the delays, pushed up to the Cannady house and began to demand that Neal be delivered up. A spokesman for the Committee of Six pleaded with the assembled people, explaining the fear that bystanders might be hurt and promising that the prisoner would be brought out from the woods when it was safe to do so.

The request did not sit well with some of the men in the mob. Alcohol was being consumed and the longer they waited, the more they drank. As tempers flared, many of the people began to reconsider their presence. One by one, people started to slip away from the farm and make their way home. In a reversal of the arrival of the crowd, its departure from the scene started as a trickle that turned into a stream that turned into a river. By 11 p.m. only the most hardcore remained. Of the 3,000 or so people seen at the farm by the *Times-Courier* correspondent earlier in the evening, fewer than 200 were still on hand by midnight.[10]

The messenger had already made his way back to Peri Landing, however, where he told the Committee of Six members about the hostile reaction of the crowd and expressed his fear that a riot would be the result if they appeared at the Cannady farm with Claude Neal. Fear, then, played as big a role as anger in the tragedy that followed.

[1] *Dothan Eagle*, October 26, 1934, p. 1.
[2] *Marianna Times-Courier*, October 27, 1934, p. 1.
[3] Howard Kester, *The Lynching of Claude Neal*, 1934, p. 2.
[4] *Jackson County Floridan*, November 2, 1934, p. 2.
[5] *Ibid.*
[6] *Dothan Eagle*, October 26, 1934, p. 1.
[7] Interviews with elderly Jackson County residents, 1982-1990.
[8] Kester, *The Lynching of Claude Neal.*
[9] King interview.
[10] *Ibid.*

CHAPTER ELEVEN

The Claude Neal Lynching

Author's Note: This chapter is based in part on interviews with two members of the "Committee of Six." These interviews were conducted for historical purposes during the early 1980s. Both men were elderly and in poor health at that time. Both are deceased today. Their names are being withheld as a courtesy to their families.

As their stress grew with the approach of darkness and the appointed time for the lynching at the Cannady place, the members of the Committee of Six began to drink. The back and forth messages and aggressiveness of the mob at the farm took time and by around 10 p.m., several of the men were heavily intoxicated. Claude Neal during this time also became more aggressive. Perhaps he saw the appointed time for the lynching come and go and watched as the men holding him drank and argued amongst themselves. Whatever his reasoning, he no longer displayed the politeness he had shown the men when they brought him back from Brewton. Neal now taunted them.

When people drink heavily, they exhibit a variety of behavior patterns. Some become light-hearted and playful, some become somber and withdrawn and some become aggressive and violent.

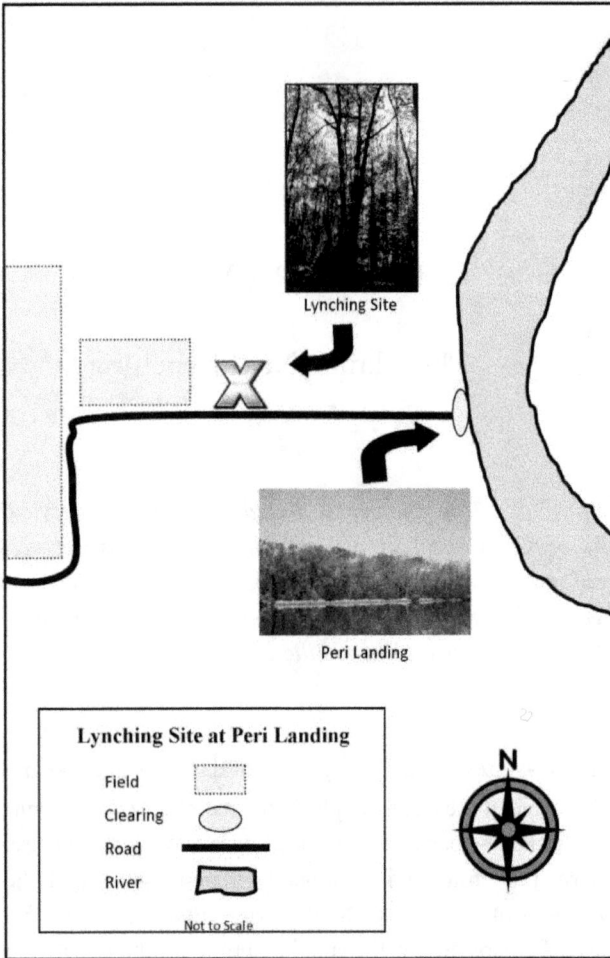

Lynching Site

Peri Landing

Lynching Site at Peri Landing

Field

Clearing

Road

River

Not to Scale

N

All three of these behaviors were exhibited by individual members of the Committee of Six. Two of the men withdrew almost totally from the debate over what should be done with their prisoner and sat quietly, taking a drink occasionally, and watching the fire burn. When pressed, one suggested that it might be best to take Neal to Marianna and turn him over to Sheriff Chambliss.

One of the other men, joking and nervous, advised taking Neal on to the farm, giving him to George Cannady and being done with it as soon as possible. He was overruled by the others.

The more aggressive members of the group became angrier and angrier as they heard Neal calling out to them as they clustered around the fire to discuss his fate. Frustrated over the situation at the Cannady farm and now unwilling to release their prisoner to the sheriff, they let their alcohol-fueled anger rise to the boiling point. The time for justice had arrived, one of them announced, and Claude Neal was going to pay for what he had done.

As the others watched, the man stood up and walked over to where Neal was chained to the tree. The man pulled out a knife as he approached, sharpening it back and forth across his pocket whetstone. For the next two hours, Claude Neal was tortured in ways that defy description.

It is not the purpose of this narrative to border on the extreme by describing each and every detail of what happened to Neal that night. As was the case in describing the murder of Lola Cannady earlier in this volume, a basic summary of what was done to the man will suffice.

The chains holding Neal to the tree were taken off, but his hands remained tied behind his back. The rope put around his neck at the Brewton jail had never been taken off and was now thrown up and through a fork in the trunk of the oak tree. One of the men pulled on the other end of the rope, lifting the struggling Neal off the ground. Another of the lynchers then approached him and used a razor sharp knife to slice a long strip of skin and flesh from his side. A hot welding torch was applied to the spot, searing Neal's flesh. He struggled wildly, his feet scrambling and reaching for the ground, his body twisting. All the while as this torture began, he was choking because the rope around his neck had been used to pull him up into the air.

It continued this way from around 10 p.m. on October 26th, until around midnight. Neal was cut and burned. The men would use the rope to pull him up off the ground until he almost choked to death, but then would release the rope to let him fall, extending his life so the torture could continue. He was beaten and strips of skin were peeled from his body.

Not all of the members of the Committee of Six took an active part in this frenzy. Two hung back, sickened by the sight but unwilling or unable to intervene. They continued to drink and would never discuss what happened that night, so long as they lived.

In the NAACP report published that same year, activist Howard Kester included what many have taken as an eyewitness account of the torture of Claude Neal. This widespread acceptance of the story is largely the result of a statement included by Kester in his introductory paragraph to the account:

A member of the lynching party with whom I talked described the lynching in all of its ghastliness, down to the minutest detail. After talking with him I went immediately to my room and tried to recall word for word all that he had told me.[1]

In a letter to NAACP head Walter White dated November 7, 1934, however, Kester said he received the account of the lynching from an unidentified man he met at random in Marianna:

...Last night I talked for one hour and forty minutes with a member of the mob which lynched Claude Neal. He described the scene in all of its horror, down to the minutest detail. I was quite nauseated by all the things which apparently gave this man the greatest delight to relate. I met him by chance and as yet I haven't been able to discover his name or address. I am doing my best to discover the leaders but I am already under suspicion and I have to move with the greatest care possible.[2]

Kester was not a trained investigator and, in fact, had never taken part in an investigation. As a result, the account he gives is suspect because there is no way of knowing whether he really talked to someone who was there. He provides no name, no description and no details at all about the identity of the man. He was, in short, some random man that Kester managed to talk to about the lynching.

Some clue to his identity was provided about two weeks later when the NAACP sent a copy of Kester's report to Governor B.M. Miller of Alabama:

...The person who gave our investigator the information...works at a Shell Oil Company filling station in Marianna and is known by the

nickname of "Red." His partner's name is Goff. "Red" said that he was present and was an eyewitness. Our investigator (i.e. Kester) asked several people... and no one of them denied it.[3]

Two members of the actual Committee of Six were interviewed during the early 1980s by this author. They provided detailed information on what was done to Claude Neal that night and the names of other men present. No one named "Red" from the Shell Oil Company station in Marianna, they were adamant, was present nor would he have been allowed even to approach the scene as they did not know him. They also laughed at the idea of any member of their group speaking to an unknown outsider in Marianna just ten days after the lynching. At that point, they said, they were concerned about the possibility of arrest and were doing everything in their power to keep their identities unknown.

The details as given by the actual lynchers differ significantly from those offered by by Kester's informant. While "Red" did provide a few accurate details about what happened that night, he also provided many inaccurate ones and told no more than was publicly known around Marianna at the time and had already appeared in numerous newspapers.

The only logical conclusion that can be reached about the account included in the NAACP report, then, is that it did not reflect an interview with an actual member of the lynch mob, but instead was a summary of much of the gossip then being told around town. It provided details that were no worse than what actually happened, but that were inaccurate when compared to information from authoritative sources.

The actual members of the Committee of Six tortured Claude Neal with increasing severity for about two hours. For as long as he was able, the man continued to talk to his torturers. He gave them details of what he had done to Lola Cannady, confessing several times (under obvious duress) that he had raped and murdered her. He tried to talk to the men in different tones, undoubtedly hoping to save his life or at least end his suffering.

The two men present said that Neal ranged from polite and submissive to angry and taunting. He would say he regretted the murder at one point, but then lash out at them and taunt them by saying that he was glad that he had committed the crime and "would do it again" if he could. None of the men of the Committee of Six, so far as is known, harbored any doubts about his guilt and the statements he made to them during the two hours of torture only solidified their conviction that he was a rapist and murderer. Neither of the living participants interviewed during the 1980s expressed any change of mind over whether Neal should have been tried in a court of law. Both felt that a trial would simply have been a "waste of taxpayer money."

The nearest neighbors to the site of the lynching lived in homes one mile or more away, but as they listened to Claude Neal's screams in the dark hours approaching midnight, they had no doubt as to what was happening. Local residents of the Parramore area said that his screams could be heard for miles around. Several residents visibly shook as they remembered the piercing sound of Neal's cries many years later. At least one hunting party of a father and his sons came up on the site, but the man left to take his boys home.[4]

As the torture continued, it became more gruesome and more severe. Neal's private parts were cut off and he was force to eat them. He was tortured in other ways as well. Finally, at around midnight, the blood thirst of the men holding him was quenched and Claude Neal was shot and killed.

The woods fell silent. Local residents that made their way to the spot the next day remembered seeing so much blood on the ground and tree that it looked as though someone had slaughtered a deer there the night before. This would have been a logical way for the people of this rural area to describe the scene, as cleaning a deer for meat was a familiar task to them. To this day they can still point out the tree where Claude Neal was killed. Some whisper in quiet asides that his ghost still haunts the spot, that nothing will grow on soil where his blood spilled and that his screams can be heard deep in the swamp on chilly nights in late October. The memory of what happened near Peri Landing that night still haunts them, in more ways than one.[5]

---

[1] Kester, *The Lynching of Claude Neal.*
[2] Howard Kester to Walter White, November 7, 1934.
[3] Walter White to Gov. B.M. Miller, November 22, 1934.
[4] Interviews with elderly Parramore area residents, 1982-1986.
[5] *Ibid.*

CHAPTER TWELVE

"Hanging from a Tree"

Even though the body of Claude Neal now lay bloody and battered on the cold ground at Peri Landing, the most hardcore members of the mob at the Cannady farm continued to linger. Word arrived there sometime after midnight that Neal was dead, but 200 or so people from the original crowd of around 3,000 waited, determined to see the body for themselves. The others had gone home, either tired of waiting or having grown fearful as the tension increased in the fields around the Cannady house.

The members of the Cannady family itself remained inside their home, unsure of what was happening and wondering if Neal would be brought to them. Just up the road at the home of Sallie Smith, the few members of Claude Neal's family remaining there also huddled inside, fearful of the night and what it might bring. They had good reason to fear.

As the news rippled through the remnants of the crowd that Neal was already dead, anger surged among the most intoxicated and/or angry of the men. Determined to be a part of exacting vengeance, they moved in mass up the dirt road to Sallie Smith's house. Seeing the torches coming, the remaining people there – including Neal's common-law wife and his young daughter – fled into the woods. The house, described as a shanty or shack by those that remembered seeing it, was burned to the ground. A member of Neal's family remembered seeing the dark shadows of chickens flying from the flames as the house burned. This memory was repeated by a white observer who did not participate in the mass arson, but saw the flames rise while standing up the road at the Cannady house. The dark forms of chickens, he said, could be seen flying through the air and away from the fire.[1]

Neal's daughter and her mother were carried across the Chattahoochee River to Donalsonville, Georgia, by a neighbor. They remained there for some time after the lynching. Not even five years old, the young girl would remember very little of what happened that night, but she retained a fear that something might happen again throughout her life.

After having waited at Peri Landing an hour or so after they killed Claude Neal, the men of the Committee of Six finally decided it was time to take his body to the Cannady family.

Based on the description of his informant, "Red," Howard Kester described a darkly brutal scene at the Cannady house:

Neal's body was tied to a rope on the rear of an automobile and dragged over the highway to the Cannidy (sic.) home. Here a mob estimated to number somewhere between 3000 and 7000 people from eleven southern states was excitedly waiting his arrival. When the car which was dragging Neal's body came in front of the Cannidy home, a man who was riding the rear bumper cut the rope.[2]

Contrary to similar reports and the claim of Kester's informant, however, the body was not dragged behind the car from Peri Landing to the Cannady farm. Neal's remains were heaved up onto the back bumper of one of the cars, the rope still around his neck, and one of the members of the Committee of Six climbed onto trunk and rode there to make sure it didn't fall off.

From Peri the car moved slowly through the woods until it reached the main road, today's Parramore Road. Once on this road it continued up to the main crossroads at Parramore and turned right onto an old road that led to the Cannady farm. A man's belt, thought to belong to Claude Neal, was found on the dirt road at Parramore the next day.[3]

Part of the route followed by the lynching party can no longer be followed today. Many roads in eastern Jackson County have been relocated over the nearly eight decades that have passed since Claude Neal was killed. The path taken by the car from Parramore to what is now the east end of Fire Tower Road no longer exists and only short traces of the original road can still be found. Modern Oak Grove Road runs roughly parallel to the original route, although a short section of the 1934 road is now a private driveway named Lawson Lane near the north end of Oak Grove. From this point to the eastern end of Fire Tower, the old road has been lost to time and pine tree farming.

From the eastern end of today's Fire Tower Road, the route of the lynching party followed that road to its intersection with Wintergreen Road. From Wintergreen it continued onto Dozier Road and to the Cannady Farm. Contrary to Kester's description of the road as a "highway" it was mostly a dirt road in 1934, and not a very good one at that.[4]

Only one of the cars made the final leg of the trip to the Cannady place. The men in the other headed for their homes. As the vehicle approached the farm, the people still gathered there saw the lights coming and surged up to the yard to see what they had waited twelve hours or more to see. Men tried to hold them back and for the most part succeeded. As the vehicle approached, the man sitting on the trunk kicked Neal's body off into the dirt. It was then dragged behind for a few hundred feet up to the front of the house where the car came to a halt. The man sitting on the trunk jumped to the ground, cut the rope and called out, "Here he is!" He then climbed into the car and the vehicle drove away into the night.[5]

Only the most determined diehards were still at the farm. Many of them were angry that they had been denied a part in the killing and could be heard yelling and cursing at the car as the last members of the Committee of Six drove away.[6]

Having heard the commotion outside, George Cannady walked onto his porch, gun in hand. Other members of his family followed behind him, although several remained inside the house. There have been a myriad of accounts of what happened next. The version told by Kester's informant, who may or may not have been present in the yard, was particularly brutal. "A woman came out of the Cannidy house and drove a butcher knife into his heart," he said. "Then the crowd came by and some kicked him and some drove their cars over him."[7]

A verifiable eyewitness, interviewed in 1986, disputed the claim that cars were driven over the body. As he recalled it, the body was left in the dust just in front of the house. With the remnants of the mob milling about and members of Lola's family watching from the porch, a relative named Edgar Pines walked from the house to Neal's body and fired several bullets from a handgun into it. This witness did not recall the butcher knife incident but did not dispute that it "might have happened."[8]

After some time was spent viewing Neal's body and discussing his fate, someone in the mob recalled aloud the efforts by Sheriff Chambliss to save the man's life by moving him from jail to jail, one step ahead of the mob. "If old Flake wants him so bad," he was quoted as saying, "then let's take him to him!"[9]

The body was hoisted onto the bumper of another car and a procession of vehicles left the Cannady farm and started for Marianna. The *Times-Courier* correspondent was an eyewitness to what happened next:

...Another mob was organized and they brought him to Marianna at 3 o'clock this morning where it hanged him to a tree on the east side of the court house lawn. His nude body was hanging at that place at an early hour this morning. After stringing him up in the tree, the mob quickly dispersed.

Neal's body was mutilated. Three fingers of one hand and two on the other had been amputated, besides other mutilations.[10]

The missing fingers and toes were not cut off by members of the Committee of Six during the actual lynching, but by the mobs at the Cannady farm and in Marianna after Neal was dead. At least one remained preserved in a small bottle of alcohol and in the possession of Marianna resident as late as 1986. It was taken as a souvenir at the time the body was hanged on courthouse square.

A more detailed account of the hanging of the body at courthouse square was provided by a now defunct news service. Based on interviews with several eyewitnesses, the reporter wrote:

A rope was fastened around the neck and willing hands hoisted the body into the tree.

As the negro's dancing feet cast fitful shadows from the glare of automobile headlights against the red brick of the courthouse, members of the mob of several hundred, which had dwindled from more than 2000 that had gone to the Cannidy farm earlier in the night, rushed upon the body with unsheathed knives and slashed the negro's body.

In the crowd were many women, some with babes in their arms, and children.

The crowd was swelled by citizens who rushed to the courthouse square when word spread of the lynching....

Some jested grimly.

"We fixed him up all right," one grim-faced farmer, shotgun in hand, remarked. "And he got what he deserved."

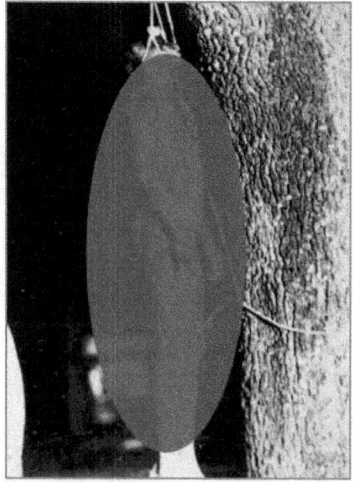

Body of Claude Neal in Marianna

Others remained silent. They came and stared and then went away.[11]

As the correspondent noted, the crowd at the courthouse vanished quickly. Sheriff Chambliss did not learn of the incident until he was awakened by a telephone call between 5 and 6 a.m. from the staff at the Baltzell Hospital in Marianna. Harrison McKinney, the bank robber shot during the escape attempt near Cottondale on the night of the 25th, had died there at around 5 a.m.[12]

Rising from bed and starting for the hospital, Chambliss drove around courthouse square and saw the body of Claude Neal hanging there. He gave the time in his report to Governor Dave Sholtz as 6 a.m.:

...Body of Neal discovered by Sheriff hanging to tree in Court House grounds. Taken down by Sheriff and taken to jail yard. Body was cold; had been dead some time. Now understand that dead body was hung there just before daylight.[13]

Parking his car and running south on Madison Street to the county jail, Chambliss called for help and Deputy J.C. Cooper and another eyewitness followed him back to the courthouse. The eyewitness remembered that the sheriff was furious and recalled him saying that, "People have gone plumb crazy!"[14]

Local journalist John Winslett received a call at about this time from a source he identified only as a downtown merchant. The man had arrived to open his business for the day just as Chambliss was running down the street to the jail. Realizing what was happening, he called Winslett who rushed to the courthouse with his camera.[15]

Winslett took the now infamous photographs of Claude Neal's body hanging outside the Jackson County Courthouse. He recalled in 1982 that he had taken several photographs of the body that morning as Sheriff Chambliss was preparing to cut it down from the tree, but had preserved only one of the negatives. The original negative was still in his possession in 1982 when he made a print from it for this author. Winslett verified the sheriff's report that the body was immediately taken down and carried into a wood enclosure that then surrounded a portion of the jail grounds.[16]

The Jackson County Jail in use in 1934 still stands as of the writing of this narrative (2011), although it is currently vacant and expected to be demolished. Later expanded, it was the facility that remained in use until the 1980s when it was replaced by the modern county corrections complex in southwestern Marianna. The building was renovated and used for a number of years as a county administrative annex.

Within two hours of finding Neal's body hanging from the tree in the center of town, Sheriff Chambliss found himself faced with yet another crisis. It was Saturday morning, the day when people who could afford to do so came into Marianna from miles around to do their weekly shopping. The crowd on this particular morning was far larger than normal, not because of the lynching but because Marianna was filled with visitors making their way home from the American Legion Convention in Miami or on hand for the Congressional District Democratic Convention and expected speech by Claude Pepper. As word of mouth spread that Neal's body had been found hanging at the courthouse that morning, a new mob formed and converged on the jail:

8:00 A.M: Marianna full of people, demanding to see body and demanding that it be hung up again; all of which was refused by Sheriff. Circuit Judge requests that crowd be permitted to view body at the jail in orderly manner, which was done.[17]

Chambliss' version of events, as quoted here, was confirmed by John Winslett and other eyewitnesses. The sheriff, according to James F. King, was adamant that the body should not be put on public display. He was angry, reported the eyewitnesses, and expressed his willingness to fire on the crowd if it attempted to storm his jail.[18]

It was at this point that Circuit Judge Amos Lewis intervened and directed that the body be displayed in front of the jail on the condition that the people in the crowd agree to walk by and view it in an orderly fashion. Chambliss refused to address the mob, but a local veterinarian agreed to do so and explained that the body would be shown so long as the people formed into single file and walked past until everyone had seen it. Shouts of agreement came back from the mob and the body was carried out of the enclosure and, over the continuing objections of the sheriff, placed on public display. The people formed into a long procession that wound its way around the block and walked slowly past. No additional mutilation of the remains was allowed.[19]

As soon as this gruesome spectacle came to an end, Chambliss ordered that Neal's body be brought back into the jail enclosure. It was then placed in a car and slipped out of town. At 10 a.m., the mortal remains of Claude Neal were buried in the clay at Nubbin Ridge Cemetery near Greenwood. The gravesite was obscured from fear that people might try to dig the body up and put it back on display.[20]

The bank robber Buford Mears was expected to be in Circuit Court for sentencing that morning, as were several other individuals, but it was decided best not to risk danger to any inmates by trying to bring them to the courthouse. As Sheriff Chambliss noted, court was adjourned for the day "on account of the mental condition of people."[21]

The "mental condition" of the people was far from resolved.

---

[1] Interview with Neal Relative, 1986; Interview with Cannady Neighbor, 1986.

[2] Kester, *The Lynching of Claude Neal*, p. 2.

[3] Interview with eyewitnesses to passage of vehicles, October 1982 and July 2010 (names withheld by request).

[4] *Ibid.*

[5] King interview.
[6] *Ibid.*
[7] Confidential informant named "Red," quoted by Kester, *The Lynching of Claude Neal*, p. 2.
[8] King Interview.
[9] *Ibid.*
[10] *Marianna Times-Courier,* October 27, 1934, p. 1.
[11] International News Service report, datelined Marianna, Florida, October 27, 1934.
[12] Chambliss, Lynching Report.
[13] *Ibid.*
[14] King Interview.
[15] Winslett Interview.
[16] *Ibid.*
[17] Chambliss, Lynching Report.
[18] Winslett Interview; King Interview.
[19] *Ibid.*
[20] *Ibid.*; Interview with Sheriff John P. McDaniel (retired), 2011.
[21] Chambliss, Lynching Report.

CHAPTER THIRTEEN

The Marianna Riot of 1934

The size of the crowd in Marianna continued to grow as more and more people, both black and white, flooded into town. Most came simply to shop or participate in the widely-publicized political events of the weekend. Others came after hearing reports that Claude Neal had been lynched and his body found hanging at the courthouse.

The planned speeches by Claude Pepper were cancelled, as was the expected protest march by the Jackson County FERA Purification League. Many of the people that had come to town for these events continued to linger, however, and eyewitnesses later recalled that a "frenzied" or "turbulent" air seemed to linger over the town. A single spark, many realized, could ignite severe violence. Concerned for the safety of their families, many mothers and fathers loaded their children into their cars or wagons and headed for home as fast as they could.[1]

The spark that many feared flared at high noon:

12:00 noon: Negro named Bud Gammons seized by angry mob of about 100 white people at Court House, which accused him of striking a white man with a bottle. Deputy Sheriff Davis rescued Gammons from mob and

91

got him into Sheriff's office on second floor of Court House. Mob storms office, demanding the negro be taken from the Sheriff and lynched. Sheriff manages to hold them off, with aid of several good citizens, Circuit Judge Lewis, Justice Buford of the Supreme Court, and others. About an hour required to quiet down this mob, and negro held in office.[2]

Exactly what happened to ignite the outbreak, as is often the case with such scenes, is not clear. Howard Kester, who did not use Gammon's name but did have good sources in Marianna's black community, wrote what is probably a reasonable account of the beginning of the riot:

Toward noon a white man struck a Negro who sought to defend himself and in the struggle with the white man, hurled a pop bottle at him. By this time a crowd had gathered and the sight of a Negro resisting a white man (threw) the crowd into a frenzy. The Negro finally tore himself away from the mob and ran across the street and into the courthouse, where he was given protection by a friendly group of white men. The mob clamored for another victim, but they were held at bay by a machine gun.[3]

The story has a definite ring of truth to it. Numerous other accounts, including reports in both local newspapers, mention the bottle throwing incident, as does the sheriff's report to Governor Sholtz. Considering the tense situation that prevailed in town at the time, it is logical that some kind of a confrontation led Gammon to throw the bottle. A local eyewitness also verified Kester's statement that the mob was "held at bay by a machine gun," although he said the sheriff did not really have one, but pretended to as he yelled down at the rioting men from his office window on the second floor of the courthouse. The ruse worked and the mob backed away from the courthouse door long enough for the men inside to organize a defense of sorts.[4]

As the Bud Gammon incident was underway in front of the courthouse, chaos also erupted at the jail. The telephone log of the governor's office in Tallahassee indicates that emergency calls from Marianna started coming in at 1:30 p.m. Eastern time (12:30 p.m. in Marianna, Jackson County is in the Central time zone):

1.30 P.M.   Cooper, Deputy Sheriff, Marianna being held prisoner in jail, mob outside, send help at once.[5]

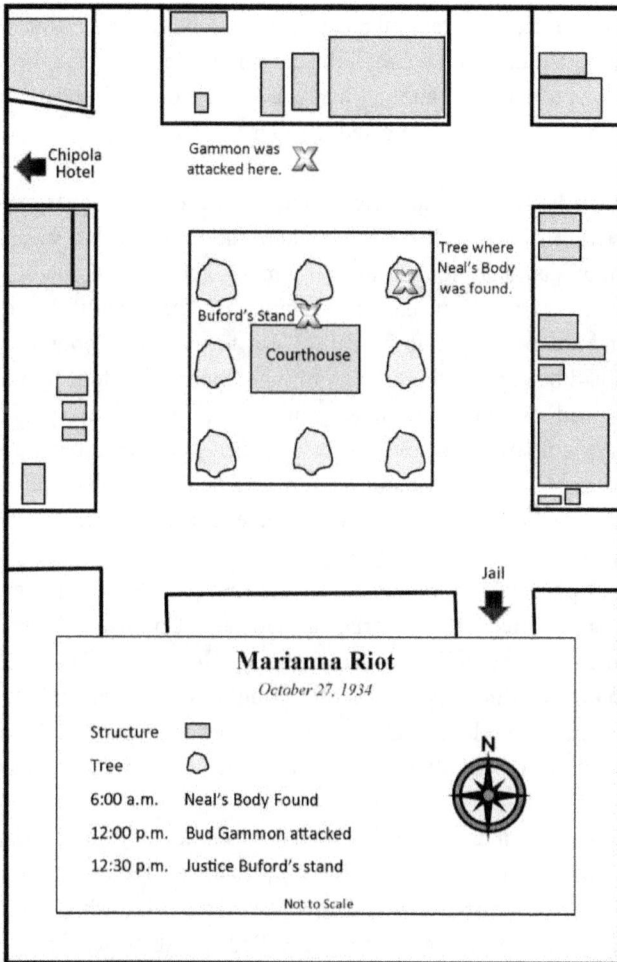

Marianna Riot
October 27, 1934

Structure □
Tree ○
6:00 a.m.   Neal's Body Found
12:00 p.m.   Bud Gammon attacked
12:30 p.m.   Justice Buford's stand

Not to Scale

The report from Deputy Cooper was the first in a rapid series of telephone calls that passed back and forth between Tallahassee and Marianna over the next 45 minutes. At 12:35 p.m. the governor's office called W.R. Smith in Marianna, trying to learn more about the nature of the outbreak underway in the city. While Smith was attempting to gather more

93

details, State Attorney John Carter called Tallahassee at 12:37 p.m., reporting that authorities in Marianna "need help – trouble due to street altercation."[6]

At 12:40 p.m., just ten minutes after the initial call from Deputy Cooper, the governor's office called the courthouse in Marianna for a status update and was told that an attempt would be made to pacify the crowd. The men defending the building promised to report back quickly.[7]

In one of the most remarkable moments in Florida history, Associate Justice Rivers Buford of the Florida Supreme Court, who was visiting Marianna that day and found himself among the men cornered in the courthouse, emerged from the front doors of the beautiful old brick structure and stunned the mob by calling out to them in a booming voice. The rioters had been preparing to batter in the door with a four by four inch post, but Buford's sudden appearance caused them to back away. His exact words remain unknown, but the justice's speech must have been powerful because the members of the mob turned away from their attempt to storm the courthouse, an effort that likely would have ended with great loss of life.

At 12:50 p.m., twenty minutes after the first plea from help came into the governor's office from Marianna, General Collins of the Florida National Guard was authorized to call out troops to suppress the violence in Jackson County. Collins reported that he would move immediately to do so, but that his men would need three to four hours to arrive. Companies of guard troops from Tallahassee and Panama City were immediately activated.[8]

Frenzied calls, meanwhile, continued to come in from Marianna as more and more people took it upon themselves to call the governor's office and plead for help. At 1 p.m., for example, Harold F. McCaskill, the head of the American Legion post at Marianna, called to ask that help be sent at once. He reported that rumor was spreading through town that Sheriff Chambliss had been killed, but promised to try to confirm the news. McCaskell was told that state troops were on their way.[9]

Four minutes later, Marianna Mayor Jhon W. Burton called Tallahassee. While he was able to confirm that Sheriff Chambliss was still alive, Burton "advised that help needed at once." He too was informed that the National Guard was on its way.[10]

Minutes after the end of the call from Mayor Burton, General Collins notified the governor's office that the companies in Tallahassee and Marianna were beginning to form. He advised that aircraft were being arranged to fly tear gas, officers and additional troops from St. Francis Barracks in St. Augustine should additional support be deemed necessary.[11]

While it is difficult to imagine, all of these calls to and from Tallahassee took place within just 45 minutes of the beginning of the Marianna riot. While the strong words from Justice Buford had backed the mob away from the courthouse doors, the violence was far from over. Sheriff Chambliss later described the scene in his report to Governor Sholtz:

12:00 – 3:00 P.M: Numerous outbreaks against negroes in Marianna, consisting of kicking them off the streets by crowds of white people, mostly drinking, and mostly from Alabama and Georgia, and surrounding counties. These mobs forced their way through several private dwellings searching for negroes, and presented themselves to numerous business establishments in Marianna demanding the negro employees. Several business men kept them out at the point of a gun.[12]

The violence that took place on the streets and in the neighborhoods of Marianna that afternoon was witnessed by many of the people in the city and numbers of elderly residents recall it to this day. The memory of the scene is so shocking to many that, while they will acknowledge having seen parts of the riot from their homes or businesses, they become too emotional to discuss it even 77 years later.

According to citizens of both races willing to discuss the riot with Howard Kester two weeks later, the scene was shocking:

*...I am reliably informed that this mob was led by a young man from Calhoun county, who has money and comes from a **good** family. The mob apparently started from the west side of the Plaza and began driving Negroes from the streets and stores where some were engaged in buying and selling and working for white employers. An observer stated that, "the mob attacked men, women and children and that several blind persons were ruthlessly beaten." Another observer said: "They (the Negroes) came from the town in droves, some driving, some running, some crying, all scared to death."[13]*

As both Kester and Sheriff Chambliss noted, white residents of Marianna stepped forward in many cases to defend their black friends, customers and employees from members of the mob. Virtually every long-established Marianna family, black or white, has stories related to the riot. Elderly black residents when asked will speak of fear, of violence, of beatings and threats that their homes and businesses would be burned. White senior citizens describe a horrible scene beyond their imagination. Many tell of how their fathers, mothers, uncles or aunts used shotguns, rifles and pistols to protect black citizens. Black residents often used knives and guns to protect themselves. The stories are best summed up by Kester:

In several instances the mob met resistance on the part of white employers of Negro labor. A Negro porter was serving a white customer in front of his employer's store. Before he knew what was happening the mob was upon him. With a knife he slashed his way through the mob and gained the front door of the store. His employer locked him in a room and kept the mob away with a shot gun. A woman who was caught downtown with her maid almost single-handedly drove the mob away from their intended victim. After emptying the streets, stores, places of business, hotels, etc., of Negroes the mob started into the residential section to drive out the Negro maids. Some women sent their maids home, others hid them in closets. One man whose wife shielded her maid from the mob said, "Saturday was a day of terror and madness, never to be forgotten by anyone."[14]

One story that is often told in Marianna today is of a woman who lived on Clinton Street between St. Luke's Episcopal Church and City Hall. Hearing that rioters were pushing into her neighborhood, she moved her black domestic employee and the woman's children into a second floor area of her home and then positioned herself on the staircase with a double-barrel shotgun. When men stormed into the house, she drove them back out with sharp words and the pointed muzzle of the gun. "I was reminded of my mother's stories of how she used a shotgun to keep out the Yankees during the Battle of Marianna," she supposedly remarked.[15]

The rioting, meanwhile, continued. At 1:18 p.m., still just 58 minutes after the initial plea for help from Deputy Cooper, American Legion head McCaskill called the governor's office to report that the situation was quieting. The Legion, he said, had considered intervening to stop the riot, but decided such an attempt was not advisable.[16]

Just eight minutes later, however, Dr. Baltzell called Tallahassee to report that the situation was still very bad, "worse than can be imagined." He urged the governor to send two companies of troops, an action that was already underway, as the rioters were "threatening to burn out all negro quarters tonight."[17]

At 1:30 p.m., ninety minutes after the start of the riots and one hour after the first call for help, Fred Davis, a key aide to Governor Dave Sholtz, called the office in Tallahassee for an update on the situation. He was told that Sheriff Chambliss had not been killed. Asking when the troops would arrive in Marianna, Davis was told that the Tallahassee company would be leaving its armory in ten minutes. The estimate was close, as the lead elements of the unit pulled out for Marianna at 1:44 p.m. Central time.[18]

As the rioting was underway in the streets of Marianna, Deputy Dave Ham died in his hospital bed in Chipley. He had courageously given his life in the performance of his duties to the people of Jackson County. Ham, it will be recalled, likely saved the life of Claude Neal at one point when he observed a caravan of cars passing through Cottondale on the evening after Lola Cannady was killed. Neal was then in the Bay County Jail in Panama City and Ham's intuitive phone call reporting what he had seen gave Bay County officers just enough time to get the prisoner on a boat and out of town before the mob arrived prepared to storm the jail. Dave Ham was by all accounts a good, fair and tough lawman. His name is inscribed on the monument to fallen officers at the Jackson County Sheriff's Department.

In a turn of events that Ham himself would have opposed, news of his death immediately spread through the mob which responded with calls for even more violence:

1:00 P.M: Deputy Sheriff Ham dies in Chipley of wounds inflicted by Mears.

2:00 P.M. Lots of talk about lynching Mears for killing Deputy Ham. Mears moved from Chipley to Panama City for safe-keeping; and brought back to Chipley at 9:00 P.M.[19]

The blows striking Sheriff W.F. Chambliss, Justice Rivers Buford, Circuit Judge Amos Lewis, Mayor Jhon Burton and the small group of officers, officials and citizens working with them to try to restore order seemed to increase as the minutes ticked by. The governor's phone log shows that call after call came into Tallahassee that afternoon, as officials, citizens and business people pleaded for help. At one point even the clerk of the Chipola Hotel called to report that he could see "fist fights going on." The crowd, he said, was "peeved" at the sheriff. "Surely need help," the hand-written notation of his call reads, "running all negroes out of sight."[20]

Matters were made even worse by the fact that the Marianna Police Department simply vanished. It should be noted that the city's police force in 1934 was a far cry from the professional and well-trained officers it employs today. Threatened by the mob, the handful of officers disappeared from view:

During the rioting the city of Marianna was completely without police protection. I was told that members of the mob searched the town for members of the police force and threatened to beat them up if they were found. One observer said, "The United States army couldn't have stopped that crowd Saturday morning." When Mayor Burton realized what was going on and that the city was at the mercy of the mob, he tried to locate the policemen but was unable to do so.[21]

Burton, it was claimed, tried to find and deputize men willing to serve as policemen to help in the emergency. The crowd was so large and so out of control, however, that he was unable to find anyone interested in sacrificing his life or health in an effort to confront the mob.[22]

As the rioting and violence went on, unsuspecting visitors continued to arrive in Marianna. Many of these guests were American Legion members making their way home from their convention in Miami. Marianna and Jackson County had invested heavily in a marketing campaign to bring people into the city as they came and went from the convention to their homes in other states. Among the groups arriving in Marianna that afternoon was a much publicized Chevrolet Caravan:

Arrangements have been made for the stopping here, on the return trip from Miami, of a motorcade of 75 cars, containing 250 Legionnaires, who will spend the night of October 27. Entertainment will be provided, sleeping quarters will be furnished, and every effort made to give the visitors a favorable impression of Marianna.[23]

The *Floridian's* statement that every effort would be made to give visitors a "favorable impression of Marianna" seems almost surreal today. People making their way home and hoping to stop in Marianna for the night arrived to find a riot in progress and talk of a lynching on every set of lips. Jackson County's dream of a weekend that would launch a new era of progress and prosperity evaporated into the October air.

In an almost surreal moment, the seventy-five cars of the Chevrolet Caravan pulled into Marianna shortly before 4 p.m. The sight of so many men in uniform arriving in so many vehicles sent a shock through the rioters. They believed, it is widely said in Marianna today, that National Guard troops had arrived in the city. The crowd pulled back to see what was going on and most of the violence came to an end.

At 4:30 p.m., four and one-half hours after rioting erupted in Marianna, troops of the Florida National Guard arrived in the city. The arrival of the Legionnaires in their Chevrolet Caravan had already stunned the mob, but the appearance of the guardsmen stopped it in its tracks.

News that soldiers had arrived flowed through the mob like electricity. The timing of the appearance of the guardsmen was fortuitous, as there was general agreement among officials and eyewitnesses that the rioters were preparing to move on the neighborhoods populated primarily in those days by Marianna's black citizens. Everyone not involved in the mob feared the results of an orgy of violence and burning that would likely follow.

The deployment of the troops to Marianna took place with remarkable speed and efficiency. From the moment orders were given by Governor Sholtz to call out the Guard, the men took up positions on the streets of Marianna in less than four hours. Considering that National Guard members serve part-time and had to be assembled, equipped and transported, the companies from Tallahassee and Panama City deployed that day with a speed and efficiency that present-day military officers find remarkable.

Machine guns were posted on the corners of courthouse square, positions that gave the gunners long views down all of the approaching streets. Officers set up their headquarters in the courthouse where they conferred with the sheriff, judges, mayor and other officials about the situation and what needed to be done. Based on these conversations, troops were deployed to patrol the town and to guard key points including both the courthouse and the jail.

Clearly intimidated by the firepower and determination of the guardsmen, the last vestiges of the mob disappeared. After a day of noise and violence, residents remembered that an eerie silence settled over the city. The violence had ended in literally a single minute. Other than soldiers, officials and deputies, no one moved. The debris-strewn streets were empty and most of the citizens – black and white – huddled in their homes waiting to see what might happen next.

There was initial fear that the mob might reorganize and return, but it did not, although there were rumored threats that it would return the following Saturday to complete what it had started. There were some sporadic fights one week later, but the riot was over and Marianna was now an occupied city.

Considering the nature and scope of the riot, it was literally a miracle that no one was killed. Several people were injured and Bud Gammon had been assaulted and nearly lynched, as had the unidentified employee of a local store, but no additional deaths took place. No estimate was ever prepared of the extent or value of the damage caused by the rioters. Whatever the total, it was miniscule compared to the damage done to the reputation and economic dreams of Marianna and Jackson County.

---

[1] Stories of being in town that morning and being told to "load up" by parents for quick departures are commonly told by elderly residents of Jackson County.

[2] Chambliss, Lynching Report.

[3] Kester, *The Lynching of Claude Neal*, pp. 2-4.

[4] King Interview.

[5] Phone Log of Governor's Office for October 1934, Florida State Archives.

[6] *Ibid.*

[7] *Ibid.*

[8] *Ibid.*

[9] *Ibid.*

[10] *Ibid.* (Note: Burton's name was spelled "Jhon" not "John" as given by McGovern and other writers.)

[11] *Ibid.*

[12] Chambliss, Lynching Report.

[13] Kester, *The Lynching of Claude Neal*, p. 4.

[14] *Ibid.*

[15] Often repeated Marianna tradition about the riot.

[16] Phone Log of Governor's Office for October 1934, Florida State Archives.

[17] *Ibid.*

[18] *Ibid.*

[19] Chambliss, Lynching Report.

[20] Phone Log of Governor's Office for October 1934, Florida State Archives.

[21] Kester, *The Lynching of Claude Neal*, p. 4.

[22] *Ibid.*

[23] *Jackson County Floridan*, October 19, 1934, p. 1.

CHAPTER FOURTEEN

The Occupied City

Despite the worst fears of many local residents, the night of the riot passed more quietly than expected. The National Guard soldiers from Tallahassee and Panama City patrolled all areas of the city by car and moved about the vicinity of the courthouse on foot. There were threats of violence in some areas of the city and rocks were thrown at houses of black residents, but no outbreak took place and no additional injuries were reported. About two dozen black residents expressed fear for their lives and were brought to the courthouse by the soldiers and allowed to sleep there.

Although historian James R. McGovern, writing in his book *Anatomy of a Lynching*, described the temperatures that night as hot and told how soldiers and citizens alike tried to sleep in a sweltering courthouse with the windows closed, climate data actually shows that the weather was cool. As far south as St. Petersburg, in fact, the lowest temperatures of the fall were recorded.[1]

Rain moved into Jackson County during the night of October 27-28, 1934. Many local citizens who lived through the riot still credit this change in the weather with suppressing additional violence. The rain kept more people home and off the streets, allowing the situation the time it needed to cool down.

The news coverage of what had happened in Jackson County, however, was just beginning to heat up. People across the nation picked up their newspapers on Sunday morning to read accounts of the Claude Neal lynching and the violence that had swept through the Florida town that many had never heard of and others knew only for its popular Satsuma oranges. It was the beginning of a media tidal wave that would continue for years to come.

Readers of *The New York Times*, for example, learned on Sunday that National Guard troops were standing guard in the streets of Marianna and that anti-lynching organizations were calling on President Franklin D. Roosevelt to invoke the Lindbergh Kidnapping Law and order Federal prosecutors to pursue the men involved in the lynching. There was no comment from the president.[2]

On the Pacific coast, readers of the *Seattle Daily Times* learned how Vivian Stubbs had stood down a group of rioters determined to seize black employees of a café by telling her they could have them only over her dead body. The same article described how Marianna auto dealer J.J. McCaskill stood with a shotgun in the door of his business to save his black employees from being taken by the mob. Sheriff Chambliss, the paper reported, was protected by a bodyguard of National Guard soldiers because he had infuriated the rioters by not delivering up Bud Gammon to them.[3]

The New Orleans *Times-Picayune* reported on Sunday that machine guns pointed out from each corner of courthouse square while 120 heavily armed members of the Florida National Guard watched for any sign of trouble. It also carried details of the lynching, although the site was misidentified as being near the Chipola River instead of on the Chattahoochee where it actually took place. This error was widely repeated in other papers.[4]

In Texas, the *Dallas Morning News* reported that Mrs. John M. Hanna, a Dallas resident and the chairperson of the Texas Council of Southern Women for the Prevention of Lynching, had already dispatched a letter to U.S. Attorney General Homer S. Cummings calling for a federal investigation of the lynching. He was urged to "use the full power of your department to apprehend and punish the murderers" of Claude Neal.[5]

And in Portland, the *Sunday Oregonian*, published an article on the riot beneath a headline that read, "LYNCHING BEE HALTED." The reference was to the intervention of the Florida National Guard to stop the outbreak before other people could be killed.[6]

Hundreds of other newspapers around the world published similar stories as wire service reports flooded out from Marianna. Reporters flooded into the city on Sunday and the flow of stories originating from the city continued throughout the coming week. Some were accurate, some were not and some were a mix of truth and rumor. All were troubling. Sheriff Chambliss for the most part refused to talk to any of the media representatives that made Marianna their temporary home for the next few days. He did confirm for several that Neal had confessed to the murder of Lola Cannady and also told others that the lynching would be investigated.

His real focus on Sunday, however, was the funeral of his slain deputy. As National Guard troops stood at attention, David H. Ham was laid to rest at Pope Cemetery in Sneads:

Funeral services were held at the Methodist Church at Sneads on Sunday afternoon at three o'clock, with Rev. A.B. Tanton officiating. Interment was in Pope cemetery, and the rights were attended by a large number of sorrowing friends and relatives. Active pallbearers were Roy Monk, S.E. Parker, H.E. Hall, G.E. Bagley, A.A. Cawthon and L.H. Cartledge. Honorary Pallbearers were Sheriff W.F. Chambliss, deputies Walter Davis, J. Robinson and Cooper, County Judge D.H. Oswald, and S.A. Tharp.[7]

The *Jackson County Floridan* described the 36-year-old Ham as "an efficient, fearless peace officer." He was survived by his wife, Lucy, and their two children, Leonard and Agnes. Buford Mears, the bank robber charged with killing the deputy, had been returned to Jackson County by National Guard soldiers at 1 a.m. that morning.[8]

As peace continued to prevail in Jackson County, the soldiers removed their machine guns from view to encourage a return of normalcy to the city. There were rumors and rumblings that more violence could break loose at any minute, but nothing happened. Such rumors would continue for weeks. With the situation clearly calming by late afternoon, the Panama City troops were dismissed and ordered home. The Tallahassee men remained to provide protection for the citizens that night and to assist with court security the next day. The night was peaceful and quiet. Rain again started to fall across Jackson County on Sunday afternoon and continued through the evening. It helped the continued calming of the situation by keeping people indoors and off the streets.[9]

On Monday morning, October 29th, soldiers ringed the interior of the circuit courtroom with their rifles at the ready as other guardsmen brought the surviving Malone bank robbers, Mears and Dudley, from the nearby jail for their sentencing:

With a military escort, Buford Mears and M.F. Dudley, convicted of armed robbery charges in connection with the hold-up of the Bank of Malone, were brought into court here Monday morning, at which time Judge Amos Lewis sentenced them to life imprisonment. Only a small crowd was present, and no disturbance marked the occasion.

Anticipating a public demonstration against Mears and Dudley, a number of soldiers, members of the National Guard Company which was called to Marianna Saturday afternoon, were stationed at strategic points about the courtroom, but their presence proved unnecessary.[10]

As might have been expected under the circumstances, Judge Amos Lewis declined to set bond for Mears. A $10,000 bond was set for Dudley. Surrounded by soldiers, the two men were escorted to waiting vehicles and taken to the Washington County Jail in Chipley.[11]

Determined to head off any additional violence in the city, Major Jhon Burton issued a statement calling on the citizens of Marianna to join him in assuring that law and order were respected and that city ordinances were firmly carried out:

"Due to recent occurrences in the City of Marianna, in which there was exhibited an unruly spirit and a disregard for law and order, and
"WHEREAS; Marianna has always been a peaceful and law-abiding city, and
"WHEREAS: Unfortunate circumstances have made necessary a proper exhibition of the majesty of the law with full enforcement of the same, and
"WHEREAS: Our good and law-abiding citizens should be assured of the upholding of their constitutional rights, now therefore,

I, Jhon W. Burton, Mayor of Marianna, by virtue of the authority vested in me, do hereby declare that law and order will be adequately and fully preserved and respected in the City of Marianna;

That the law-abiding citizens will be properly safeguarded;

That all laws and ordinances on the statutes of the City of Marianna, particularly those covering drunkenness and rowdyism, will be strictly and rigidly enforced so that the peace of the City will prevail on all future occasions.

Furthermore, I hereby call on all law-abiding citizens to do everything possible to help me fully sustain the peace of the City and to render justice without fear or favor.

JHON W. BURTON, Mayor.[12]

The mayor was clearly shaken and embarrassed over allegations that city police did not do their duty during the riot. In a meeting with the Marianna Merchants Association the following week, he went so far as to be "governed by the wishes of the Association" with regard to Saturday police protection for coming weeks:

We have added two policemen for regular duty, one for day duty and one for night duty in addition to the regular force which we have maintained. This plan will be in operation at least until the end of the year. Considerable criticism of Marianna's night patrol has come to me and I cannot say that it is true, but I wish the people not to overlook the fact that the city has not the funds necessary to maintain an adequate force also I request that criticism of the department be withheld unless well-founded.[13]

Criticism over what Marianna police officers did or did not do during the riot however, would continue for more than seventy years. Burton provided an interesting explanation of why city policemen had not responded more aggressively in an interview with a reporter from the *Dothan Eagle*. "I had only two policemen," he said, "to send them against that mob meant probable injuries and death for somebody; what I did was tell them to circulate among the crowd." They were instructed to "spot the leaders for later arrest" while using what influence they could to hold the mob "back as well as they could."[14]

It is a strange explanation for the inaction of the Marianna Police Department, but has a ring of truth to it. How well the two officers carried out the mayor's orders is impossible to say. The mob was so big and so out of control that there was little that two men could do to interfere. If any of the leaders of the crowd were identified per the mayor's instructions, none were ever indicted or prosecuted by the local grand jury.

The investigation of the lynching began while the Tallahassee National Guard unit was still in town. As tempers cooled and questions could be asked, Sheriff Chambliss and his remaining deputies began an effort to obtain more information about the killing. Circuit Judge Amos Lewis ordered the Jackson County Grand Jury to convene on Monday, November 5th, to investigate such matters as it thought appropriate. Obviously, the killing of Claude Neal and murder of Deputy Dave Ham would be the primary focus of the grand jurors.

As local authorities began the first stages of their investigation, Colonel J.P. Coombs of the Florida National Guard also made an inquiry into the circumstances of the lynching and subsequent riot. The commander of the troops sent to Marianna, Coombs did what he could to learn what had happened and who was involved. The results of his brief investigation would be made public in coming days.[15]

In Tallahassee, as the national media continued its detailed coverage of the situation in Marianna, both criticism and support flooded into the office of Governor Dave Sholtz. The general gist of these letters, calls and telegrams was that the governor should have done something to stop the lynching. He promised a full investigation and summoned Sheriff Chambliss and State Attorney Carter to appear in his office.[16]

A friend and ally of President Roosevelt, Sholtz had proclaimed on the very day of the lynching that Florida was about to enter the greatest decade in its history. He was determined that the growing tide of outrage over the lynching would not attach itself permanently either to himself or his state.

W.L. "Bud" Gammon, the man that had nearly been lynched by the mob on Saturday, was released from the Jackson County Jail on Monday afternoon. He had been held there for his own protection, but Sheriff Chambliss allowed him to go at 1 p.m., "after ascertaining that he would be safe at home." He would later be called to testify before the grand jury as it investigated the lynching and riot.[17]

With the situation now calm enough for local authorities to resume control, the National Guard soldiers from Tallahassee boarded buses to go home. They left Jackson County as darkness fell on the evening of October 29, 1934. The military occupation of Marianna was over.[18]

---

[1] James R. McGovern, *Anatomy of a Lynching*, pp. 92-93

[2] *The New York Times*, October 28, 1934, p. 1..

[3] *Seattle Daily Times*, October 28, 1934, p. 1.

[4] New Orleans *Times-Picayune*, October 28, 1934, p. 13.

[5] *Dallas Morning News*, October 28, 1934, Section I, p. 14.

[6] *Sunday Oregonian*, October 28, 1934, p. 2.

[7] *Jackson County Floridan*, November 2, 1934, p. 1.

[8] *Ibid.*

[9] *Panama City Pilot*, November 1, 1934.

[10] *Jackson Conty Floridan*, November 2, 1934, pp. 1, 8.

[11] *Ibid.*; Chambliss, Lynching Report.

[12] *Jackson County Floridan*, November 2, 1934, p. 1.

[13] *Jackson County Floridan*, November 9, 1934, p. 1.

[14] *Dothan Eagle*, October 30, 1934, pp. 1-2.

[15] *Tallahassee Democrat*, November 1, 1934, p. 1.

[16] *Ibid.*

[17] Chambliss, Lynching Report.

[18] *Ibid.*

CHAPTER FIFTEEN

The Investigations

The investigations into what happened during the ten days that passed between the death of Lola Cannady and the end of the Marianna riot started while National Guard troops were still in the streets. Peace was slowly returning to Jackson County, but the wave of outraged letters, telegrams and phone calls pouring into the Governor's office and the White House was just beginning to build. This wave soon became a tsunami.

In Marianna, at the request of Governor Dave Sholtz, Sheriff W.F. Chambliss worked to assemble what he knew about the murder of Lola Cannady and lynching of Claude Neal into a formal report. The events of the previous ten days had been so stressful and so chaotic that the sheriff was hard-pressed to even assemble a timeline of events into an understandable format. His resulting report was completed on October 31, 1934. It provided much greater detail about the events in Jackson County than many writers have claimed.[1]

The most noteworthy information included in Chambliss' written report is a detailed timeline that provides, in many cases, a minute by minute account of what happened in Jackson County during that terrible October. The eight page typewritten document is an under used resource in understanding the murders and subsequent riot. Not only does it provide an accurate timeline of what happened and when, it also details that Sheriff Chambliss did take every action possible to protect Claude Neal from the growing mob and, contrary to much of what has been written about the case, that he did investigate other suspects in the Lola Cannady murder.[2]

The details of the investigation as provided in the sheriff's report offer a strong rebuttal to the claims posed by many writers that law officers never considered the possibility that someone else might have murdered the young woman. It details the physical evidence in the Cannady murder and also proves that the initial investigation of the killing was far from being the racial prelude to a lynching that some have claimed.

The report indicates, for example, that Claude Neal went into the field where Lola Cannady was murdered not long after lunch on Thursday, October 18th, the day the woman was reported missing. He remained there for two hours, then came home, changed clothes and went to the nearby home of John Daniel where he spent the night in a corncrib. This information explains why Neal was identified as a person of interest, even before the young woman's beaten body was found in a nearby patch of woods.[3]

The sheriff clearly states that his officers also "checked up on the whereabouts of a white man named Calvin Cross, who was under suspicion." If it had been the intent of Chambliss or his deputies to "railroad" Claude Neal, why would they have done this? Cross was able to provide an alibi and was cleared of suspicion in the murder.[4]

The report also indicates, however, that deputies were equally as willing to clear a black person implicated in the murder as they were a white. When Neal confessed his involvement in the murder, he initially implicated a second black man named Herbert Smith in the crime. If Jackson County authorities were handling their investigation from a racial perspective, they could have easily accepted Neal's word and charged Smith as a co-defendant in the murder. They did not.[5]

Instead, the sheriff immediately questioned the claim because it did not match with the physical evidence. Instead, according to the report, he urged Sheriff Gandy of Pensacola NOT to let Neal sign a written confession implicating Smith until his officers were able to talk to Smith. They cautiously picked up Smith and slipped him out of the county to Tallahassee and eventually to Brewton to confront Neal about the allegation. When

Claude Neal saw him, he immediately recanted the part of his confession having to do with Herbert Smith and admitted that he had committed the crime alone.[6]

In the case of Herbert Smith, Sheriff Chambliss and his deputies worked hard to clear a black man accused of involvement in the rape and murder of a white woman. Using Claude Neal as a key witness, they could have easily charged and tried Smith in the murder, but instead they cleared him. Again, this is a clear indication that the sheriff was not interested in prosecuting Neal simply because of his skin color. This is highly significant because to this day many claim without evidence that Claude Neal was arrested simply because of his race.

The sheriff initiated his investigation anticipating that he would be called to testify before the Jackson County Grand Jury. Circuit Judge Amos Lewis had already summoned the grand jurors to convene at the courthouse on Monday, November 5th to investigate new matters (i.e. the Claude Neal lynching). Because he was already looking into the lynching, Chambliss was able to assemble his report quickly when he and State Attorney John Carter, Jr., were called to Tallahassee by Governor Dave Sholtz.

The meeting took place at the Governor's Office in Florida's historic Old Capitol building on November 1, 1934. Chambliss presented his written report to the governor, but also delivered an oral report, as did State Attorney Carter. Both men answered questions about the Cannady murder, Neal lynching and Marianna riot. After a lengthy discussion, the three men emerged to discuss the investigation and case with reporters.

Rumors were floating that there might be further violence in Jackson County on the coming Saturday night (November 3rd), but Chambliss was quick to tell the gathered media representatives that it would not be allowed to happen. He had sworn in extra deputies, he said, promising that the first man who showed even an inclination of causing trouble would find himself in jail.[7]

Turning to State Attorney Carter in front of the gathered reporters, Sholtz gave what many interpreted as an order for a thorough grand jury investigation:

We don't condone lynching in Florida. I want you and the grand jury to make a vigorous and thorough effort to run down the ring leaders of this mob and prosecute them. It has been reported here that some of the ringleaders are supposed to be known.[8]

The request was not really an order, as the Florida Constitution does not allow the governor to give orders to local grand juries. The Jackson County Grand Jury had already been summoned to meet on the matter, so it was more of a public reinforcement of what Carter was doing than it was a direct order from Sholtz.

Much has been made of Sholtz's statement that "some of the ringleaders are supposed to be known." It is tempting to use this statement as support for a claim that the identities of at least some of the men of the Committee of Six that lynched Claude Neal were known to both local and state authorities. Carter's brief notes of the Tallahassee meeting, however, indicate otherwise. He states clearly that the three men "discussed rumored leadership of mob of 27th." This confirms that Sholtz's statement referred not to the lynchers, but to the leaders of the Marianna riot that followed Neal's murder. These men had not been involved in the actual lynching.[9]

As Chambliss had foreseen, there was no second outbreak in Marianna on the first Saturday after the riot. There were some rumblings, but nothing of consequence and the city remained peaceful. Fear and worry would continue for a number of weekends to come, but the risk of dramatic new violence faded with each passing Saturday.

The *Jackson County Floridan's* weekly issue came out on the day after the meeting of the two local officials with the governor. In addition to wide-reaching coverage of the events of the previous week, it included a front page column titled "Lynch Law." While most historians and writers researching the lynching have assumed it was written by the state attorney of that name, the author was probably John Carter, Sr., his father and a local historian that sometimes wrote columns for the paper.

After a somewhat detailed history of the practice of lynching, it warned that the only way for such crimes to end was for citizens to feel confident that justice could be obtained through the courts. The writer insinuated, however, that the furor over the Scottsboro case may have had much to do with the fate of Claude Neal:

In the South, in Reconstruction days, lynching was resorted to as swift punishment for crime, and is with us today. But it is now confined practically to one offense, and only one punishment, death. As hard as we try to wipe it out, it remains with us. It is going to remain, undoubtedly, until civil government is made stronger, and public sentiment is educated up to demand legal punishment only for all crimes. It is one thing to say, "Let the law take its course" and another for men to stand emotionless in the presence of a crime that staggers humanity. Lynch law is deplorable. But civil institutions must be greatly strengthened before they will supplant the lynching evil. Lynch law is a challenge to the weakness of legal procedure. If the Scottsboro, Ala., case is a living example of "the law taking its course," the outlook for the suppression of lynch law any time soon, is dismal.[10]

The Scottsboro case had been major news since 1931, when authorities in North Alabama arrested nine young black men on charges that they raped two teenage white girls. In a situation that was eerily similar to the Marianna riot, a mob formed and demanded the accused be turned over to them for lynching. The sheriff refused and called the governor who sent in the Alabama National Guard. Machine guns were placed at the courthouse in Scottsboro, just as they would be three years later in Marianna.

The trials of the suspects, who became known as the Scottsboro Boys, went forward. Eight of the nine were convicted of rape, which was then a capital offense in Alabama. They were sentenced to death and the Alabama Supreme Court upheld the convictions on appeal. The U.S. Supreme Court, however, reversed the convictions because the justices did not feel the defendants had received proper access to competent legal counsel during their trials. The men were retried, this time with a legal team provided by the American Communist Party. The Scottsboro Boys were again found guilty. Their cases were again appealed. And once again the convictions were overturned.

When the Claude Neal lynching and Marianna riot took place in 1934, the nation was waiting to see what would happen when the men were tried again a third time the following year. They would ultimately be convicted again. One of the men escaped and did not serve prison time, finally being pardoned by Governor George Wallace in 1976 after he was found living a secret life in Brooklyn, New York. The others went to prison, although the four youngest were soon released by the state.

Scottsboro was a name on every Southerner's lips in 1934. Many white people below the Mason Dixon Line were outraged that local juries and the Alabama Supreme Court had been overruled at that point not just once, but twice. They were wary of the Communist Party and its allies in the Socialist Party that were making the Scottsboro case a *cause celebre'* against the South and the ability of its citizens to serve impartially on juries considering the fates of black defendants. They were particularly irate that two young girls had been gang raped and had testified against the men who raped them, but that the convictions of the men kept getting overturned. Most black Southerners, in turn, believed that the Scottsboro Boys were innocent and saw signs of hope in the actions of the justice system.

In the North, the Scottsboro case played into superiority sentiments about white Southerners that would be magnified by what happened in Jackson County in October of 1934. Southern people, the conventional wisdom in the North and in liberal movements held, were inherently racist and could not be trusted to administer fair and impartial justice in cases when black individuals were on trial.

When Lola Cannady was found raped and murdered, the name "Scottsboro" loomed over the South like a dark cloud, regardless of one's point of view. The rural people of northeastern Jackson County were determined that the Lola Cannady murder would not become a new Scottsboro case. When enough evidence was accumulated to, in their minds, eliminate other suspects and put the blame for the crime on the head of Claude Neal, there would be no need for trials and appeals. Justice, according to one member of the Committee of Six, would be served quickly and irreversibly. He believed that the Scottsboro case had not prevented lynchings, but had caused them.

The Jackson County Grand Jury convened on the morning of Monday, November 5, 1934. It would be the most significant session of the grand jury since the days of Reconstruction when the county was caught up in a blood bath remembered still today as the "Jackson County War." Not only would it consider the Claude Neal lynching, but also the murder of Lola Cannady, the Marianna riot and the murder of Deputy Dave Ham.

Circuit Judge Amos Lewis gave the grand jurors what the *Jackson County Floridan* described as one of the most forceful charges in the history of the county:

The Grand Jury, which was recalled by Circuit Judge Amos Lewis, received one of the strongest charges in the history of this county, and is expected to make a thorough investigation of the recent lynching of Claude Neal, who was removed from the Escambia county jail at Brewton, Ala., and supposedly put to death by an armed mob near Greenwood on the night of October 26. The Escambia county (Ala.) grand jury is also scheduled to begin an investigation on the removal of the negro from the jail at that place, and Sheriff W.F. Chambliss has been called to appear before that body when it begins its work on Nov. 19.[11]

The parallel grand jury investigations resulted after Alabama's governor learned through the newspapers that Neal had been seized from the Brewton jail. He requested that the Escambia County (Alabama) Grand Jury investigate thoroughly and do everything possible to bring those responsible to justice. The Jackson County grand jurors, however, met first.

Had the media reported widely on Judge Lewis's charge to the grand jury, even more protest mail would have flowed into the Governor's Office in Tallahassee. In speaking of the murder of Lola Cannady, he is said to have remarked:

A more diabolical crime could not have happened between the pearly gates of Heaven and the depths of Hades than when one of our fair young women was brutally murdered, and the sentiment which prevailed (during the lynching) is the same which predominated among our forefathers in the southland.[12]

The initial day was spent conducting relatively quick investigations into other crimes requiring grand jury consideration. Buford Mears was indicted on charges of First Degree Murder in the death of Deputy Dave Ham. A first degree murder indictment was also returned against Frank Pope, a convict on a county "work gang" who had contributed to the general chaos by cutting Silas Griffin to death near Sneads on October 30th.[13]

Serious indictments also were returned against Van Cox and Oscar Phillips. Both white, they were accused of attacking Wallace Campbell during a Halloween night burglary. No trial date was set.[14]

The jurors then recessed until Wednesday when they returned to begin their investigation of the murders of Lola Cannady and Claude Neal. They returned their report to Judge Lewis two days later:

117

We have not been able to get much direct or positive evidence with reference to this matter; practically all of our evidence and information being in the nature of hearsay and rumors. However, we find that Miss Lola Cannidy (sic.) was brutally raped and murdered in this County on the 18ᵗʰ day of October, 1934, by Claud Neal, a negro, and that Claud Neal came to his death in this County on the 26ᵗʰ day of October, 1934, at the hands of a small group of persons unknown to us, after being forcibly removed from the jail at Brewton, Alabama, about 175 miles from here, by persons unknown to us.[15]

The grand jurors had discovered what Sheriff Chambliss already knew: no one was talking about who had killed Claude Neal. Those with knowledge of what had happened simply declined to tell what they knew. The names of the members of the Committee of Six and the Peri Landing location of the lynching were closely guarded secrets. As one of the six lynchers would say nearly fifty years later, the sheriff and grand jury could investigate until the sun refused to shine, but they were not going to learn any details about what had happened to Claude Neal and who had done it.

The grand jurors seem to have been aware that a veil of secrecy had descended over the entire affair. They also agreed that Sheriff Chambliss had done all that had been possible for him to do to save Claude Neal from the mob:

We find that the Sheriff of this County did everything within his power under the circumstances to protect his prisoner, and we commend him for his action in performing his duty.

We do not think anything can be accomplished by remaining in session longer at this time, but we are ready and willing to continue our investigation of this matter at any time additional evidence of a convincing and substantial nature can be presented to us.[16]

There is in the records of the Jackson County Circuit Court a curious note that probably has to do with the grand jury's investigation of the lynching and subsequent riot. It shows that 22 witnesses testified before the grand jury during its investigation of a murder attributed to "John Doe." Among the names on the list are those of Deputy Walter Davis, W.L. "Bud" Gammon, W.H. Ham (an apparent relative of Deputy Dave Ham) and others. They were unable to identify the name of a murder suspect and returned a No True Bill in the case.[17]

The Escambia County, Alabama, Grand Jury would hear testimony and review evidence in the case as well, trying to identify the men responsible for taking Claude Neal from the jail in Brewton. Sheriff Chambliss was among those that testified before the panel, but as was the case in Jackson County, the Alabama grand jurors could not penetrate the veil of secrecy that surrounded the lynching. No fault was found to rest on the shoulders of Sheriff Byrne or his deputies, but otherwise the panel simply could not find the evidence it needed to indict or prosecute any of those responsible for the taking of the prisoner.

Although much criticism was later aimed at authorities in both Jackson County and Tallahassee for not sending in National Guard troops to save Claude Neal from the lynch mob, officers of the Florida Guard were insistent that they could have done nothing even had they been summoned in time.

In an appearance before the Florida Cabinet on November 1st, the same day that Sheriff Chambliss and State Attorney Carter met with Governor Sholtz, Lieutenant Colonel Percy Coombs of Apalachicola said there was virtually nothing the troops could have done. No one knew where Claude Neal was being held, Coombs told the cabinet members. And with Jackson County covering over 900 square miles and no one even sure if Neal was inside the county at the time, he doubted that his men would have had any success in finding the small group holding him somewhere deep in the woods.[18]

Coombs was probably right. The Florida National Guard was an effective military force, as it would prove in World War II, but it was neither intended nor trained for the mission of finding a handful of people hiding from it in a vast rural area. Even had the entire state force been sent to Jackson County on the 26th, it would have had only a few hours to find Neal. The possibility of his murder being prevented by the military was virtually zero.

The various governmental investigations into the Claude Neal lynching failed to penetrate the secrecy with which the Committee of Six had surrounded itself. The result was that neither the Florida nor the Alabama

119

grand jury was able to identify or return indictments against the men that actually raided the Brewton jail and lynched Neal. Rumors and innuendo abounded, as the Jackson County Grand Jury had noted in its presentment, but hard facts were few and far between. Law enforcement in Jackson County would occasionally ask questions, but no answers were ever uncovered.

The end result of the process was that sufficient evidence had existed to indict and try Claude Neal for the murder of Lola Cannady, but that the suspect had been murdered by persons unknown before such a trial could take place. And while rumors had abounded over the leadership of the riot in Marianna on October 27, 1934, the grand jury could not find sufficient hard evidence to return an indictment.

The shadow of Scottsboro remained long on the land.

[1] Chambliss, Lynching Report
[2] *Ibid.*
[3] *Ibid.*
[4] *Ibid.*
[5] *Ibid.*
[6] *Ibid.*
[7] *St. Petersburg Times*, November 2, 1934, Section 2, Page 3.
[8] Manuscript notes of John H. Carter, Jr., November 1, 1934, Slade West Collection, see also numerous newspapers November 2-3, 1934, including *St. Petersburg Times*, November 2, 1934, Section 2, Page 3.
[9] Manuscript Notes of John H. Carter, Jr., November 1, 1934.
[10] "Lynching" by John H. Carter, *Jackson County Floridan*, November 2, 1934, p. 1.
[11] *Jackson County Floridan*, November 9, 1934, p. 1.
[12] Undated clipping, ca. November 5, 1934, Slade West Collection.
[13] *Jackson County Floridan*, November 9, 1934, p. 1.
[14] *Ibid.*
[15] Jackson County Grand Jury Presentment, November 9, 1934, Jackson County Archives.
[16] *Ibid.*
[17] Grand Jury Docket Book 3, p. 8, Jackson County Archives.
[18] *St. Petersburg Times*, November 2, 1934, Section 2, Page 3.

CHAPTER SIXTEEN

Howard Kester's Investigation for the NAACP

On October 31, 1934, Walter White, the chief secretary of the National Association for the Advancement of Colored People (NAACP), wrote to Howard Kester, a Virginia born Socialist, requesting that he travel to Marianna as quickly as possible:

We would like to get all the gruesome details possible together with any photographs of the body, crowd, etc., and as much evidence as is possible as to the identity of the leaders and members of the mob.

As the capacity of the American people for indignation is great but short-lived, get the facts to us as soon as you can, won't you?[1]

Kester was an interesting choice to head the organization's private investigation of the Claude Neal lynching. He had no investigative experience or training. In fact, prior to being contacted by White about traveling to Marianna, he had most recently been an unsuccessful candidate for a seat in the U.S. Congress on the Socialist Party ticket.[2]

Born in 1904 near Martinsville, Kester was 12-years-old when his family moved to the coal town of Beckley, West Virginia. It was there, in a state that had left the South and joined the North during the Civil War, that he was exposed for the first time to the Ku Klux Klan. Spending his teen years in Beckley had a formative impact on Kester. He observed firsthand the strife between management and labor in the coal fields and was heavily influenced by the philosophy of the United Mine Workers of America.

He left Beckley for Vanderbilt where he majored in divinity but, perhaps more than anything else, studied socialism. He was one of the leaders in the movement for what today is called social justice. According to his own memories, Howard Kester became the front man of the NAACP's investigation of the Claude Neal lynching almost by accident.

He was, he told interviewers 40 years later, an admirer of Walter White and often stopped by to visit White when he was in New York. White liked the young man. The NAACP's national secretary, however, was heavily involved in the Scottsboro case when the Claude Neal lynching took place in 1934. He needed someone willing to go to Marianna and take a look around and since Kester was, as he stated it, foot loose and fancy free, White asked him if he would go. Thirty years old and with an interest in pushing the cause of social justice in the South, Kester agreed.[3]

Contacts with Marianna's black community were arranged for him with assistance from NAACP members in Tallahassee as well as students of what was then Florida Agricultural & Mechanical College (today's Florida A&M University) in that city. A black minister in Marianna agreed to try to meet with Kester when he came to town and a tentative meeting was set at a local church.[4]

Kester's account of his time in Marianna is somewhat confusing. In one part of his interview for the University of North Carolina's Southern Oral History Program he said that he was almost lynched there. He described walking from the Chipola Hotel to the nearby church where he was to meet the minister and some of the elders, but said he fled from the meeting when he saw a number of people searching with flashlights. He assumed they were looking for him and went back to his hotel, entering through the kitchen to avoid being spotted from the plaza.[5]

No one locally has any recollection of a second lynch mob during the first and second weeks of November, when Kester was in Marianna. In fact, as Sheriff Chambliss had told the media in Tallahassee, he had deputized extra officers and was prepared to make arrests at the first hint of trouble. The Marianna Police Department had also hired additional officers. Local leaders were determined that there would be no more violence largely because of the economic impact the riot and the subsequent coverage of the lynching was having on the city. It is hard to imagine that a mob could have been roaming Marianna with flashlights looking for Howard Kester and that no one would have noticed it.

In fact, Kester himself did not say that he knew for a fact the people he saw with flashlights were after him. He only assumed they were and this opinion was bolstered when a filling station employee that had been one of his primary sources told him "they" were out to get him. Kester told interviewers in 1974 that he did not wait to learn the truth of the rumor, but left Marianna for Nashville within 30 minutes. He never reported feeling threatened to either the sheriff or city police officers.[6]

Whatever the people were doing in the dark with flashlights, the truth is that Howard Kester's presence in Marianna was pretty well known, as was the fact that he was staying at the Chipola Hotel. During his visit, which lasted only a few days, he generally roamed around the city collecting rumors and talking to anyone he could find actually willing to talk to him. Local officials and residents were suspicious of him, but really weren't overly concerned. Marianna was still the temporary home of a large number of out of town reporters and Kester was treated about as they were, politely but cautiously. Out of town reporters are still treated that way in Marianna if their topic is controversial.[7]

Kester confirmed this when he told interviewers that he roamed around Marianna for several days, eating hamburgers in local diners and talking with citizens. Some, he found, enjoyed discussing the lynching and subsequent riot. Others did not.[8]

So far as can be determined, Howard Kester never interviewed nor did he try to interview Sheriff Chambliss, Deputy Coulliette, Malone Constable Hall, State Attorney Carter, the doctors that examined Lola Cannady's body, the members of the coroner's jury, or really anyone else in a position of authority with the possible exception of Mayor Jhon Burton. Nor did he try to talk to Sheriff Harrell in Washington County, Sheriff Byrne in Brewton or similar lawmen in Pensacola and Panama City. He did not talk with the county solicitor that witnessed Neal's confession in Brewton or any of the inmates of the jail there. He did not talk to Neal's mother or great-aunt about what they observed. He did not visit the Cannady farm and did not try to talk with Lola's family, even though they were fairly accessible to anyone that wanted to talk to them.

Kester was not a trained investigator and apparently the idea of going to the scene of Lola Cannady's murder never occurred to him and while he reported rumor about Herbert Smith, the man originally implicated by Neal as a participant in the murder, he never went to Malone to interview Smith, even though he had already been released from protective custody and was back home.

Basically, he did what local residents remembered him doing and what he himself said he did. He roamed around town and talked to people. His primary informant, in fact, was a man named "Red" who worked at the local Shell Oil Company gas station. "Red" (Kester never gave his real name) claimed that he was at the Cannady farm on the night of the lynching. He very well may have been there, but the information gleaned from him by Howard Kester did not coincide with the statements of other eyewitnesses.[9]

As a result, Kester recorded a lot of rumor and innuendo about the lynching, with information from an occasional eyewitness in the mix. It is remarkable considering the brief time he spent in Marianna and his lack of effort to talk to key figures in the lynching and related events that Howard Kester's final report has been used as a definitive source by so many of the people writing about the incident.

In fact, the primary value of Kester's final report and of a preliminary letter he wrote to Walter White on November 7, 1934, is that they provide good insight to the "street talk" going around in Marianna a week or two after the lynching. Much of that same street talk can be heard today.

In his preliminary letter, for example, he described how he stumbled across one of the men involved in the Claude Neal lynching:

...Last night I talked for one hour and forty minutes with a member of the mob which lynched Claude Neal. He described the scene in all of its horror, down to the minutest detail. I was quite nauseated by the things which apparently gave this man the greatest delight to relate. I met him by chance and as yet I haven't been able to discover his name or address. I am doing my best to discover the leaders but I am already under suspicion and I have to move with the greatest care possible.[10]

The man that talked to Howard Kester appears to have been identical with "Red," his informant at the local Shell station. He was definitely not one of the men that actually killed Claude Neal, although he could have been one of the thousands in attendance at the Cannady farm on the night of the 26th. If so, he apparently left before Neal's body was finally produced, as his account for the most part is wildly contradictory to the statements of people known to have been present that night.

Few writers have relied on Kester's preliminary letter to Walter White and as a result, few have taken notice of his most startling statement:

> *There is little room for doubt that Neal actually killed Lola Cannidy (sic.) but no evidence at all that there was any rape. Of course there could be no rape since they had been having sexual relations for some time. Claude Neal and Lola grew up together as children. They played together. Neal worked for Lola's father, Mr. Cannidy (sic.), on his farm. Lola and Neal have for some time been having intimate relations with each other. This relationship has extended over a period of months and possibly years. Recently Lola became engaged to a white man and she wanted to break off her relations with Neal. She asked him to meet her so that she could talk everything over with him. Lola told Neal not to speak to her again and if he did that she would tell the white men in the community on him. Then she told Neal that she wanted to "quit" and "would tell on him," he "got mad" and killed her.[11]*

The statement by Kester that there was "little room for doubt" that Claude Neal had actually killed Lola Cannady has been almost universally ignored by writers exploring the lynching. His claim that Claude and Lola had a relationship, however, has become almost accepted fact over the eight decades that have passed since he first raised the possibility.

How Howard Kester knew either statement to be true is open to serious question. He never talked to members of the coroner's jury, the sheriff, Lola Cannady's family, Claude Neal's family, neighbors of the two individuals or either of the doctors that examined her body. He never visited the crime scene nor did he examine the physical evidence in the case. As a result, his conclusions about the crime were based entirely on local rumor. He had no way of knowing conclusively or even with authority whether Claude Neal had killed Lola Cannady or whether the woman had been raped. And since he never visited the farm, talked to anyone in the community or interviewed members of either family, he also had no way of knowing whether there had been any kind of relationship between the two.

In fact, the description of the "meeting" that Kester asserts took place between Neal and Cannady bears no resemblance at all to Neal's actual confessions. The suspect made no claim at all that he had a relationship with Lola Cannady. He told Sheriff Gandy of Pensacola, Sheriff Byrne of Brewton and pretty much anyone who would listen that he saw her walking across the field from her home to the hog pen; that he went to the pen and propositioned her but that she refused and when he became insistent, she said, "I'll tell my daddy!" This is a very different description of what happened than the one repeated from rumor by Howard Kester.[12]

Further evidence of the questionable reliability of the information obtained by Kester can be found in his statement regarding Neal's implication of Herbert Smith in the murder:

...He tried to implicate another man by the name of Hubert Smith with whom he had had a fight the Saturday previous. Both were arrested and taken to the woods and questioned. Finally Neal told the officers that he alone was guilty and they (the officers) let Smith go. Smith is now near Malone. This is straight. I got it from prime sources.[13]

The "prime sources" relied upon by Kester could not have been too prime as 1) he incorrectly gave Herbert Smith's name as "Hubert," and 2) Smith and Neal were not arrested at the same time. The two men were not questioned in the woods together and Smith was kept in protective custody for some time after confronting Neal at the Brewton jail. About all that is right about Kester's information regarding Smith is that Neal did implicate the man, but that law officers cleared him of any involvement in the crime. He was at his home in Malone when the activist visited Marianna, but Kester was content to rely on gossip and hearsay and made no effort to go to Malone and actually talk to Smith.

The most sensational part of Kester's letter to White is his account of the actual lynching of Claude Neal as obtained from an alleged eyewitness. This supposed eyewitness statement was repeated in the final draft of the NAACP report and has been widely quoted ever since as an actual account given by one of the lynchers.

While the statement as given in its earliest form does include some accurate details, so much of it is inaccurate that its reliability as a primary source is seriously impeached. Even simple and easily verifiable parts like the distance from Greenwood to the lynching spot are incorrect. For example, Kester's "participant" told him that Neal was taken into the woods "4 miles from Greenwood." The actual distance from Greenwood to the lynching tree at Peri Landing is in excess of 15 miles.[14]

Passing over Kester's graphic description of how Neal's private parts were cut off, which all sources agree actually happened, the account as given by his "witness" continues as follows:

"...They then sliced his sides and stomach with knives and began cutting off fingers and toes." A red hot iron was used "to burn him from top to bottom." They tied a rope around his neck and drew him up in a tree where they would hold him until he almost choked to death then they would let him down and begin the process of torture all over again. Neal's body was literally cut to pieces by small wounds. After about twelve hours of torture, "they decided to just kill him." He was tied by a rope to the back of a car and dragged through two lanes of cars on either side of the highway. (It is estimated that from 4,000 to 7,000 people from all over North Florida and S.E. Alabama were on hand for the lynching) and when the car which was pulling Neal's body got in front of Cannidy's (sic.) house a man on the rear bumper cut the rope. "Mrs. Cannidy (sic.) came out and drove a butcher knife through his heart." "Then the crowd came by and some kicked him and some drove their cars over him."[15]

The actual events of that night were given in an earlier chapter, but to summarize, Neal's fingers and toes were not cut off by the Committee of Six, although some were removed by people at the Cannady house and later by the group present when his body was hanged from the tree at the courthouse. He was burned with an acetylene torch, not a "red hot iron." He was tortured for a couple of hours, not twelve, although the torture was indeed brutal and the shorter time made it no less severe. The body was not "dragged through two lanes of cars on either side of the highway" from the scene of the actual lynching to the Cannady farm. It was actually carried on the back bumper. Thousands of people had indeed been at the farm earlier in the evening, but by the time the body was produced fewer than 200 remained, not "4,000 to 7,000." None of the other witnesses described Mrs. Cannady coming out and driving "a butcher knife through his heart." And none of the other witnesses described people driving cars over the body.

A comparison of the statements of Kester's alleged member of the mob and those from people known to have been there can lead to only two primary conclusions: 1) that Kester's informant was right and everyone else was wrong, or 2) that Kester's informant wasn't really there and was merely repeating gossip for the out of town visitor.

The list of inaccuracies in the November 7th letter does not end there. Kester told White that, "I have it from the most authoritative sources that certain 'prominent business men and leaders from the best families' were in the mob." It is certainly possible that there were some well-known people from Marianna at the Cannady farm that night, but most were busy in town due to the influx of American Legion visitors, concert and the eagerly anticipated political events set for the next day. Much more suspect is Kester's statement regarding how the Committee of Six learned of Neal's whereabouts. "It is known that a business man of Marianna arranged with a party in Pensacola to have word sent here the moment Neal was released from there," he wrote. "The word was received here and a group of men set out for Brewton immediately."[16]

In fact, the men determined to bring Neal back to George Cannady did not learn that he was in Brewton via such shadowy means. They heard it on the radio in a wire service report.

Kester's statement regarding general opinions about the lynching is likely accurate. "Very few people with whom I have talked resent the lynching at all," he wrote. "Most of them think it was not only justified but that those doing the lynching should be congratulated."[17]

This was indeed a commonly-expressed sentiment about the lynching in 1934 and actually reflects something of the opinion of quite a few citizens of Jackson County today. While most people in the county agree that Neal should have been allowed to go to trial, opinions about whether he was guilty or innocent remain divided primarily along racial lines. Whites more often than not believe that Claude Neal murdered Lola Cannady. Blacks generally think that he was innocent.

As Kester was prone to do, he blamed the entire affair not on murder or racism, but on economics and the plight of the poor. Poor whites, he wrote, resented poor blacks because jobs were few and far between. He even mischaracterized the nature of Wankard Pooser's Jackson County FERA Purification League, claiming its primary purpose was to purge the Depression era relief rolls of black citizens:

The basic factor in this whole beastly affair is economic. Jackson county's population is about 50% Negro. In Marianna it ranges from 45 to

50%. There has been constant agitation on the part of the disinherited white element for the jobs of the Negroes. Employers who give work to Negroes when white men could do the work are boycotted and threatened. A sustained effort has been made to get all Negroes off the relief rolls and turn the relief entirely to the whites. A semi-Fascist organization called the "Purification League" headed by W. Pooser has been doing the most of the agitation. Pooser combines race hatred with a few of Huey Long's ideas about dividing up the wealth....[18]

The economy was very bad in Jackson County, as it was across the nation. The Great Depression was raging but on the weekend of the Claude Neal lynching, there were signs of better times on the horizon for Marianna. For the six men involved in the actual lynching, however, the issue was the rape and murder of a young woman, not the economy.

As for the Jackson County FERA Purification League, Pooser and his followers did not need to purify the relief rolls of blacks. The people operating the program were already doing that. The 1930 census data, for example, showed a total of 607 emergency relief workers in the county. Only 43 of those were black.[19]

Wankard Pooser was actually about as far removed from being a "semi-Fascist" as FDR was from being Joseph Stalin. Pooser was much more in line with Huey Long and similar populist leaders than he was with Hitler and the Nazis. He opposed government waste and he and his followers felt too many "fat cats" were holding down government relief agency jobs, diverting money that should be going to the poor and needy. He also vehemently denied that his group wanted poor blacks removed from the relief rolls. These denials were made six days before Kester's preliminary report to Walter White.[20]

Howard Kester's observations were refined over the next couple of weeks. Some of the conclusions he made in his preliminary report to Walter White were softened. Others were expanded and toughened. This was part of the preparation of Kester's final report, which would be published just three weeks later by the NAACP under the title, *The Lynching of Claude Neal.* The primary purpose of the publication, in addition to increasing public awareness of the evils inherent in lynching, was to provide extra power to the push for the passage of a national anti-lynching bill. Although Southern senators would eventually carry out a successful filibuster of the bill, the Neal case was the *cause celebre'* of the effort to pass it. The NAACP report would play a prominent role in the use of the case as a focal point of the anti-lynching law effort.[21]

The final version of Kester's report was released in published form by the NAACP on November 30, 1934. It included basically the same information as his November 7th letter to Walter White, which additional quotes from newspapers that covered the lynching. Unfortunately, Kester made no additional effort either in person, by mail or by telephone to confirm or substantiate the information he used. As a result, the final version is rife with errors, as was his preliminary report. It is, as was noted earlier in this chapter, primarily a compilation of the rumors that swirled in Marianna during the weeks after the lynching.

Following a brief appeal from NAACP secretary White for the passage of the Costigan-Wagner anti-lynching bill, the report began with a summary of the events leading up to the lynching. Errors surface in the first paragraph and continue throughout the document.

In the first paragraph, for example, Kester repeats his claim that Neal was "taken in custody with another man (i.e. Herbert Smith) whom investigating officers believed to be in involved in the murder to the woods and questioned. It is alleged the confession was wrung from Neal and that he assumed entire responsibility for the crime." The problems with this statement, as noted with regard to the preliminary report, are obvious. Smith was not arrested until three days after Neal and there was no way that investigators could have taken them "to the woods" for questioning. The allegation, which is widely repeated even today, was false.[22]

The first paragraph of the report also lists Sallie Smith, with whom Claude Neal lived, as his aunt. She was actually his great-aunt.[23]

After making this incorrect assertion, Kester goes on in the final report to detail the efforts by law enforcement to save Neal from the growing mob. After providing excerpts from a couple of newspaper articles about the events following his arrest, he quoted his own November 7th letter to White as support for the allegation that "a prominent business man of Marianna arranged with friends in Pensacola to notify him the moment that Neal was moved." With regard to Sheriff Gandy in Pensacola, he asserted that moving Neal to Brewton was "equivalent to handing him over to the mob."[24]

The writer continued by expressing his opinion of the decision to move Neal. "It would seem that had the officers been really concerned with the safety of their prisoner that they would have either held him in Pensacola or taken him to Mobile or some other large town," Kester wrote. The activist, however, did not actually talk to Sheriff Gandy or he would have learned that the Brewton jail was actually much newer than the Pensacola jail. Gandy simply did not believe that his own jail could withstand an assault by a determined lynch mob. Kester also made no effort to talk to Sheriff Byrne in Brewton, or he would have learned that not only had Byrne himself stood down the mob at one point, he would have discovered that Neal was cautioned at one point by Byrne to stop confessing the murder of Lola Cannady to fellow inmates.[25]

Since he did not actually talk to Sheriffs Gandy or Byrne, Kester relied on the Associated Press for his description of the storming of the jail in Brewton. Like the wire service reporters, he claimed that 100 men stormed the jail. The actual number of men that took Neal from the jail, however, was twelve.[26]

In the second page of his final report, Kester included the account of the lynching he obtained from "Red" at the Shell station in Marianna. As noted earlier in this chapter, "Red" might have been at the Cannady house that night, but he was definitely not present when Neal was lynched at Peri Landing and his description of the actual killing represents rumor at best, fabrication at worst. Some of its details are accurate, some are not.[27]

The bottom of the page begins a description of the riot of Marianna. Because Kester spent his entire visit to Jackson County in Marianna, he was able to talk to a number of witnesses to the actual riot. Because this was the most thorough part of his inquiry, his descriptions of the riot itself are fairly accurate.[28]

The third page of the NAACP report consisted of sixteen clipped headlines from newspapers across the country, arranged beneath the heading, "All of America Knew of Lynching in Advance." No reference is made to the fact that most of the newspapers used in the composite actually repeated a single wire service report. The fact that most of the newspapers were published one day after the lynching also is not mentioned. Only a handful of newspapers – those with afternoon editions – ran stories on the actual day of the lynching and while they repeated the obvious – that the men that took Neal from the Brewton jail planned to lynch him – none of them carried invitations for the white public to attend.[29]

On page four, Kester continued his account of the riots. Again, it includes valuable statements from people that witnessed the riot. It includes incorrect information, however, when it states that the National Guard units sent to suppress the outbreak came from Apalachicola. Only the commander, Colonel Coombs, was from Apalachicola. The actual units were from Tallahassee and Pensacola. Once again, the writer might have obtained valuable information had he tried to talk to the guard commander, but he did not.[30]

On the fifth page, which includes the graphic photo of Claude Neal's body hanging from the tree on courthouse square, Kester repeats his assertion that a fight had taken place between Herbert Smith and Neal on the Saturday prior to Lola Cannady's murder and that the two men were taken into the woods and questioned by investigators. Unfortunately, he made no effort to go to Malone and actually talk to Smith, so the claim about the fight is second hand rumor at best. The allegation that the two men were taken into the woods, as has been noted, is completely false. Neal was nowhere near Jackson County when Smith was taken into custody and carried to Tallahassee by Deputy Phil Coulliette.[31]

Under the subheading "Was Claude Neal Guilty?" Kester gave his opinion of the murder. While he had gathered no new information since his preliminary report of November 7th, he softened his overall opinion of Neal's guilt in the murder of Lola Cannady. Where he had written on the 7th that there was "little room for doubt that Neal actually killed Lola Cannidy (sic.)," now, just a few days later as the report was prepared for publication, he changed his wording to "I still have some doubts in my mind."[32]

In the same paragraph, the writer mentioned a rumor that a white man had actually killed Cannady and then taken his bloody clothes to Smith's house to have them washed. Kester noted that he could find no support for this theory among the black residents of the Greenwood area, a curious statement since he did not actually travel to Greenwood in person. He may, however, have talked to some citizens from that area that he encountered in Marianna.[33]

The source of this allegation was actually a letter sent to the NAACP offices in New York from two NAACP leaders in Bonifay, Florida, on November 5, 1934:

I am anxious that the NAACP push the matter as it relates to the most horrible and uncalled for lynching which taken place near Marianna,

Florida a few days ago. I think that I voice the sentiment of a large number of people when I say that an innocent man (Claud Neal) has been lynched. It was reported that clothes with bloodstains on them were found at Neal's home, thus causing him to become the object of suspicion and lynching. It is said that those clothes are retained in the jail at Marianna and they are not Neal's clothes. It is said that the white man who killed the white girl in question sent those clothes to Neal's to be washed by his mother.[34]

The letter writers, J.M. Carson and E.P. Sanchez, cautioned that "these may or may not be facts, but they deserve an investigation." Neither man, however, contacted the Jackson County Grand Jury or any other authorities to report the information, probably because they had no firsthand information and simply were passing along a rumor making the rounds in Bonifay.[35]

The most graphic words and descriptions in the NAACP report, however, paled next to the included photograph of Claude Neal's body hanging in Marianna. This photograph, for nearly 80 years, has formed the basis of local and national memory of the lynching. Most residents of Jackson County today know little if anything about the Neal lynching and many do not recognize his name or that of Lola Cannady. They do know about the photograph, which locals usually refer to as the "Courthouse hanging."[36]

The photograph of Claude Neal hanging at the Jackson County Courthouse has been widely reprinted and can be found on numerous websites. Howard Kester claimed in the NAACP report that the "photographer made post cards of this picture which were sold in large quantities at fifty cents each." This claim is, in fact, one of the most widely accepted allegations made by Kester against the people of Jackson County and has been repeated by innumerable writers since 1934.[37]

The photograph used in the report was taken by John Winslett, a Marianna journalist, publisher and business owner. The original negative was still in his possession during the 1980s. According to Winslett, the photograph was used in the NAACP report and has been used in numerous other publications since 1934 in violation of his copyright and without his permission. As the holder of copyright to the photograph (and several similar ones), Winslett legally owned all rights to it. In an interview with the author, he said he never filed a formal complaint or lawsuit in the matter, even though the use of the photograph without his permission constituted a violation of federal law.[38]

In the interview, Winslett also denied that the photograph was ever reproduced by anyone in Marianna as a post card and further disputed the claim that he sold copies for 50 cents each. In his words, "I could have become a rich man if I did, but I did not." According to him, the post card claim was a total falsehood. He did make a few copies, he said, for the mayor, the sheriff and a few other key people in the community. A handful of friends also talked him into making copies, but Winslett emphatically denied that the photograph was ever publicly sold on the streets of Marianna.[39]

The photographer's statement regarding the image likely explains why original copies are very difficult to obtain today. There are copies in the private collections of people around Jackson County, but when compared with prints made from Winslett's original negative, it is obvious that they were copied from other sources, possibly decades after the events of 1934. Despite the claim that hundreds of postcards of the photograph were sold in Marianna, the author has never been able to find even one, despite years of searching. Howard Kester also had trouble finding one of the photographs, even though he was in Marianna just one week after the Claude Neal lynching and at a time when, according to his own account, they had been sold on the streets in large numbers for 50 cents each:

The photo of Neal's body was difficult to secure as Mayor Burton had asked that the photographs not be shown. Most of them had been disposed of and the people who had one or more would not part with them. I offered from 50¢ to $5.00 for one.[40]

It cannot be conclusively said that prints or postcards were not sold in Marianna during the week after the lynching, but it can be said that original prints are extremely rare and that the photographer that took the image denied the claim.

Kester devoted the final pages of his report to economic issues, not a surprising turn for a Socialist politician. He slammed the education level in Jackson County, although the school system was then among the more successful in the state, and claimed that *"Time, The American Magazine, Cosmopolitan, Literary Digest, Red Book* represent about the best available reading material to be purchased in the town." The activist clearly did not take much time to learn about Marianna's real history as it had one of the most active cultural communities of any small town in Florida. Not only had the city been home to acclaimed writers and novelists, it boasted an orchestra, debate society, book club, garden club, regular stage productions and more. Even Wankard Pooser and the Jackson County FERA Purification League, which Kester unfairly cast as a "semi-Fascist" organization, held plays and worked to make sure that school teachers received their due pay and that school construction monies were spread across the county.

Kester repeated his inaccurate claims that the Purification League was a racist organization that wanted black citizens taken off the government relief rolls. In fact, the opposite was true. Pooser and his followers wanted more of the budget of FERA distributed to poor and suffering citizens – white and black – instead of being absorbed as administrative costs by the agency. Had the writer talked with Pooser in person, he might have found they were not that far apart in their view of the suffering of the poor farmers and laborers in the South.

In the closing paragraph of his final report, Howard Kester listed five conclusions he had reached about the lynching:

1) *The Mob intended to lynch Claude Neal from the beginning.*
2) *That the nature of the press reports confirmed their intention.*
3) *That the statements occurring in the local press incited to lynching.*
4) *That the local officials and the Governor of the state must have been aware of the probability of lynching, and*
5) *That insufficient protection was given to the prisoner.*

The first two conclusions were obvious. The group of men making up the Committee of Six absolutely did want to lynch Claude Neal from the beginning and did everything in its power to get possession of him. And Kester is correct, this was widely reported in both the *Jackson County Floridan* and the *Marianna Times-Courier*.[41]

His third conclusion that the local newspapers "incited to lynching," is highly questionable. This was a volatile accusation with regard to the local media and a reading of both local newspapers during the week that passed between the murder of Lola Cannady and the killing of Claude Neal reveals that while both gave the events heavy coverage, neither encouraged a lynching. The *Floridan*, in fact, ran editorial comments praising Sheriff Chambliss for his efforts to prevent a lynching and urging calmness with the statement that one crime (i.e. the murder of Lola Cannady) was enough.

The fourth conclusion, that local officials and the Governor were aware of the "probability of lynching" is partially true. They were definitely aware that a group of men wanted to lynch Claude Neal, but steps had been taken to protect the prisoner and the sheriff in particular did not think a lynching was probable at all. It was not until Neal was taken from the jail in Brewton that everyone recognized a lynching had become likely.

The fifth conclusion, that "insufficient protection was given to the prisoner," is simply not true with regard to Florida authorities. They made every effort to protect not only Claude Neal, but his aunt and sister, Herbert Smith, Buford Mears and Bud Gammon. Neal was moved from Chipley to Panama City and from there to Pensacola and finally to Brewton as part of an intense effort to protect him from the lynch mob. In Brewton, Sheriff Byrne did everything he could to save Neal, but the men from Jackson County were able to decoy him out of position and raid the jail with guns and dynamite. The Escambia County, Alabama, Grand Jury determined that no fault could be placed on Byrne or his deputies.

The reader can make his or her own conclusions about the validity of Kester's two reports. The documents did contain numerous errors, contradictions and inaccuracies. Both the preliminary report and final report are based on gossip and "street talk" that he picked up while walking around Marianna. It is remarkable that writers since 1934 have regarded them as the definitive sources of information on the lynching.

---

[1] Walter White to Howard Kester, October 31, 1934, Papers of the NAACP, Part 7, Series A, Reel 9.

[2] Interview with Howard Kester, July 22, 1974, Interview B-0007-1. Southern Oral History Program Collection (#4007), UNC-Chapel Hill (Hereafter Kester, UNC Interview).

[3] *Ibid.*
[4] *Ibid.*
[5] *Ibid.*
[6] *Ibid.*
[7] Interviews with Roy Beall, Sr, and John Winslett; Author's personal observation and conversations with key community leaders in 2010-2011.
[8] Kester UNC Interview.
[9] Walter White to Governor B.M. Miller of Alabama, November 22, 1934, Papers of the NAACP, Part 7, Series A, Reel 9.
[10] Howard Kester to Walter White, November 7, 1934, Papers of the NAACP, Part 7, Series A, Reel 9.
[11] *Ibid.*
[12] Confession of Claude Neal, Gov. B.M. Miller Papers, Alabama State Archives; Statements to various newspapers by Sheriffs Byrne and Chambliss, October 1934.
[13] Kester to White, November 7, 1934.
[14] Kester to White, November 7, 1934; Distance calculated using 1934 Highway Map of Jackson County, Florida.
[15] Kester to White, November 7, 1934.
[16] *Ibid.*
[17] *Ibid.*
[18] *Ibid.*
[19] U.S. Census for Jackson County, Florida, 1930.
[20] *Sarasota Herald-Tribune*, November 1, 1934, p. 30.
[21] Howard Kester (name given as "anonymous" in published report), *The Lynching of Claude Neal*, November 30, 1934.
[22] Kester, *The Lynching of Claude Neal*, p. 1.; Chambliss, lynching report.
[23] *Ibid.*
[24] Kester, *The Lynching of Claude Neal*, p.1.
[25] *Ibid.*
[26] *Ibid.*
[27] *Ibid.*, p. 2.
[28] *Ibid.*
[29] *Ibid.*, p. 3; Review of newspapers included on page two of the NAACP report.
[30] Kester, *The Lynching of Claude Neal*, p. 4; *Jackson County Floridan*, November 2, 1934, p. 1; Governor's Office phone log, October 27, 1934; Chambliss, lynching report.
[31] Kester, *The Lynching of Claude Neal*, p. 5; Chambliss, Lynching Report.

[32] Kester, *The Lynching of Claude Neal*, p. 5.

[33] *Ibid.*

[34] J.M. Carson and E.P. Sanchez to William Pickens, November 5, 1934, Papers of the NAACP, Part 7, Series A, Reel 9.

[35] *Ibid.*

[36] Based on casual conversations by the author with more than 100 residents of Jackson County, February – June, 2011.

[37] Kester, *The Lynching of Claude Neal*, p. 5.

[38] Winslett Interview.

[39] *Ibid.*

[40] Howard Kester to Walter White, November 13, 1934, Papers of the NAACP, Part 7, Series A, Reel 9.

[41] Kester, *The Lynching of Claude Neal*, p. 8.

CHAPTER SEVENTEEN

The 2011 Investigation

It has been called the "last spectacle lynching" in U.S. history. In October of 2011, as news rippled out that the Federal Bureau of Investigation was looking into the seventy-seven year old case, the *St. Petersburg Times* even ran a massive expose on the crime under the headline, "Spectacle."[1]

The Claude Neal lynching was a gruesome affair, but despite such claims, it was neither a "spectacle" lynching nor was it the last "spectacle lynching" in the United States, or even in Florida. Lynchings involving much larger mobs continued for years after the Claude Neal murder, and they did not always take place in small towns.

In 1935, a large mob in Fort Lauderdale lynched a sharecropper named Reuben Stacy and posed for a photograph by his mutilated body. Seven children can be distinctly seen in the image. That same year in Tampa, a mob took three socialist labor leaders from the jail to beat and then tar and feather them. Two survived but one died. Seven Tampa police officers were later accused of being in the mob. In 1938, the *Socialist Call* newspaper even bemoaned the election of Senator Claude Pepper as an "ok of lynchings." Pepper had never participated in a lynching, but he was castigated by many in the press because he participated in the filibuster of a national anti-lynching bill that would have given the federal government extraordinary powers to deal with such crimes in the South.[2]

Nor were such incidents confined to Florida. In Sikeston, Missouri, on January 24, 1942, a mob tortured and killed a black man named Cleo Wright who, like Claude Neal eight years earlier, was accused of assaulting a woman. In Atlanta that year, the police department was implicated in the branding of a black youth.[3]

These incidents do not downplay the brutality of the Claude Neal lynching, but do show that spectacle lynchings continued for years after Neal was killed and that large cities, including some with newspapers that sent reporters to Jackson County in 2011 to investigate the Neal killing, were not immune from such incidents.

The lynching and riot all but destroyed Marianna's dream of a positive weekend with thousands of visitors from across the country who would then go home and spread the word of what a nice and hospitable place it was to visit or live. Instead, the use of the Claude Neal case as a *cause celebre'* for the passage of the national anti-lynching law assured that the name Marianna would be synonymous with thoughts of lynching, race riots and violence. It has been a difficult image for the city to shed and it has not fully done so even today, despite the fact that it is a beautiful and friendly community.

The national anti-lynching law campaign failed. The U.S. House of Representatives did pass the bill, but the Senate did not. A group of Southern senators filibustered the bill to prevent it from coming up for a vote. Supporters of the legislation were unable to overcome the filibuster and the bill died in the Senate. Among those leading the filibuster was Senator Claude Pepper of Florida, who had been forced to cancel a planned speech in Marianna on October 27, 1934, because of the riot that resulted from the Claude Neal lynching. Most of the senators that killed the anti-lynching bill were branded supporters of lynching by elements of the national press, but in reality they opposed the practice. What they didn't like about the bill was that it opened the door for the government to intervene and seize power from local law enforcement and courts in the South when lynchings were attempted. The block of Southern senators considered this an unconstitutional power grab by the federal government and opposed the bill on those grounds.

World War II came in with the bombing of Pearl Harbor on December 7, 1941, and forever changed the American nation, Marianna and Jackson County included. The county made major sacrifices in support of the war effort. Hundreds of men of both races went off to fight and many never came home. Those who did, especially those from rural areas, came back with eyes that had seen the world. Whether they were black or whether they were white, these people came back from war knowing that the conditions under which they had lived before going to serve were no longer acceptable.

The war forever changed conditions in rural areas of the South as men came home determined that their families would live in better conditions than the ramshackle shacks in which they had come of age. Electric lines and telephone lines were extended into the rural areas of Jackson County. Housing conditions improved dramatically, schools improved and eventually were desegregated, healthcare improved and life expectancies increased dramatically. The war that wrapped itself around the world exposed men and women, both black and white, to what was possible in their own home communities. They back home and engineered the changes necessary to make Jackson County the pleasant, hospitable and progressive place it is today.

As this progress took place and as the county moved itself into the future, the Claude Neal lynching and Marianna riot became memories of the distant past. The beautiful old courthouse was torn down, much to the chagrin of many in the community, and replaced with a then modern looking facility. It has not aged well and there is talk at this writing of a remodeling project that will give it a façade more in keeping with the historic nature of downtown Marianna. The limb from which Claude Neal was hanged was cut from the ancient oak tree on courthouse square to eliminate a reminder of what had happened there. The tree still clings to life. The only trace of the limb is a healed wound in the bark of the oak. The old jail, where Neal's body was displayed after a confrontation between the crowd and Sheriff Chambliss, still stands, but there is talk now that it should be demolished as well. It was a modern facility in 1934, but aged over the years until it was no longer suitable for use as a jail. A new county correction center was built on the outskirts of town and the old jail was remodeled for use as a county administration annex. It is empty today and unless some preservation effort is launched to save it, will likely join the old courthouse as something seen only in photographs or the minds of those who remember it.

There are no historical markers anywhere in the county noting the Claude Neal lynching, the Marianna riot or the historical significance of these events. Out at the Cannady farm, the old house no longer stands. The pump where Lola Cannady was attacked is still there, although it is powered by electricity today. Peanuts and cotton now grow on the spot where her broken body was found. Horses graze in a pasture where Sallie Smith's house once stood.

Deep in the woods near the site of Peri Landing, the tree where Neal was actually lynched still stands. The trace of the old road still passes the site. The wrecked remains of a moonshine still can be found nearby. To reach the lynching tree from nearby Parramore Landing Park requires a difficult bushwhack through thick underbrush and dense woods. Very few people who know even the approximate location of the tree are still alive. An old legend holds that the spot is haunted. The screams of Claude Neal can be heard coming from the swamp on fall nights when conditions are right, say some of the old timers, and nothing will grow on the spots where his blood fell. There are bare spots under the tree, but then again there are bare spots under all old oak trees. It has something to do with tannic acid and is a natural occurrence.

By the summer of 2011, the Claude Neal lynching was regarded by most in Jackson County as an event of long ago. All of the men of the Committee of Six that carried out the lynching had been dead for years. Sheriff Chambliss, State Attorney Carter, Marianna Mayor Burton, Deputy Coulliette and Judge Lewis were all long deceased. So too were the parents, brothers and sisters of both Lola Cannady and Claude Neal. Anyone even the same age as Lola or Claude at the time of the murders would now be at least in their late 80s or early 90s. Most people still alive with any first hand memory of the events had been children in 1934.

It came as a point of some puzzlement then when the county learned that the U.S. Department of Justice had opened a new investigation of the Claude Neal lynching and that an agent from the Federal Bureau of Investigation was in the county asking questions. The FBI does not comment about ongoing investigations, but a Justice Department spokesperson confirmed that the Claude Neal case was on a list of roughly 100 Civil Rights era crimes being investigated by federal officers.

The basis for the investigation was the Emmett Till Unsolved Civil Rights Crime Act, signed into law by President George W. Bush in 2008.

The law provided authorization and millions of dollars in funding for the Justice Department to investigate "cold cases" or unsolved crimes dating from the era of the Civil Rights Movement. When the department compiled its list of such crimes, the Claude Neal lynching was the oldest case it decided to investigate. James Casey, an FBI Agent based in Jacksonville, was assigned to the Neal case.[4]

Agent Casey told officials in Jackson County that the investigation had been launched because of claims by a descendant of Claude Neal that his ancestor's civil rights had been violated and his family deprived of their real estate and other property because they had been "chased off" from their farm. From historians at the Florida State Archives he obtained copies of Sheriff Chambliss' report on the lynching and also requested all similar materials on file in Jackson County.

The problem in Jackson County is that very little material relating to the Claude Neal lynching remains on file in the courthouse. What happened to the original files, evidence, etc., is not known. Retired Sheriff John P. McDaniel, who looked into the lynching for historical purposes in 1986-1988, was told by county archivists that some material had been lost when a fire broke out in a building where boxes of old records were stored. Other material was discarded or lost when the records were transferred out of the old courthouse preparatory to the building of the current facility. Finally, until an employee was designated strictly for records care in the 1970s, anyone could come in, research and then literally carry away any record they found interesting without anyone knowing.[5]

About all that remains in the Jackson County Courthouse today regarding the Neal lynching are a few grand jury records, none of which detail specific evidence in the case. This lack of records is not a new development. Material from the Neal case was missing in the 1970s when the author did an internship in the county archives and nothing of significance has reappeared or disappeared since that time. The county archives did not even include a copy of Sheriff Chambliss' report until one was provided by the FBI.

Based on the questions he asked officials in Jackson County, Agent Casey appeared to be basing his investigation on Howard Kester's 1934 NAACP report. The reliability of this document was discussed in the previous chapter.

The descendant of Claude Neal that urged the case be investigated by federal authorities was Orlando Williams, Sr., who indicates he is a nephew of Claude Neal. Between 2009 and 2011, I received a number of email communications from Williams. The paragraphs that follow provide a sampling of the contents of those emails:

March 19, 2010

Dear Mr. Cox:

Since 1986 I have sent letter to the Justice department, the Federal Bureau of Investigation and lawyers in regards to the horrific murder of my uncle (Claude Neal), which also resulted in my family forced to change their names and being run off over forty acres of land they owned, during October 27, 1934....

On October 7, 2007 President Bush signed the Emmitt Til bill into law, (HR923) which opens the door for all cold cases in regards to hate crimes, to be investigated and prosecuted up to 1970.

As a part of this bill the Federal Government has allocated ten million dollars per year to investigate and prosecute hate crimes until 2017. During 1982 there was book written about this incident; The Anatomy of a Lynching the Killing of Claude Neal, which was completely investigated by Professor James McGovern of west Florida University. This incident appears to be in all the Federal and local Government archives...[6]

Williams was anxious for a federal investigation to be launched into the Claude Neal case. He indicated that most of Neal's relatives preferred not to talk about the incident and mentioned several times that he hoped to secure a claims bill from the Florida Legislature that would lead to the family being able to secure financial compensation for its losses.

Among the points referred to the Justice Department by Williams and being investigated by the FBI was a claim made by him that his family was deprived of their 40 acre farm in 1934 because they were driven from it during the lynching-related violence. This is a relatively new allegation in the case and warrants additional discussion.

At the time of the lynching of her great-nephew, Sallie Smith lived in a small wooden home not far from the Cannady house near Greenwood. The two homes were not directly across the road, as claimed by Kester, nor was

Smith's house on a bluff, as claimed by historian McGovern in 1982. There are no bluffs anywhere near the scene and while the two houses were close enough for the residents of each to see the other, their actual distance apart was about one-half of a mile.[7]

Mrs. Smith did not own the house in which she lived in 1934, but did hold title to 40 acres of property across the road from the house. This land included fields as well as the wooded area where Lola Cannady's body was found. The allegation raised by Orlando Williams is that the family was driven off the land at the time of the lynching, lost possession of it and that it wound up in the hands of a local white family.

The home in which the family lived was burned on the night of October 26, 1934, by part of the mob that formed at the Cannady farm. No one was injured in the attack, but the house and its contents were destroyed. Sallie and Annie Smith were in custody at the time their home was burned, but other members of the family including Neal's common-law wife and his young daughter were home. Neal's daughter was so young that she has no memories of the incident other than a couple of vague recollections, but she was told by her mother that a man helped them make their way to the home of relatives in Georgia.

Sallie Smith and her niece, Annie, were initially arrested on murder charges by Sheriff Chambliss. The elder woman admitted during questioning in Chipley that the bloody clothes she was found washing belonged to Claude Neal and that she had seen him approach Lola Cannady near the hog pen and then heard the young woman scream. After the riot and lynching, State Attorney John Carter took mercy on the women and decided not to prosecute them as accessories in Lola's murder. So far as is known, their alleged involvement in the crime was never presented to the Jackson County Grand Jury.

Sallie and Annie Smith had no means of support, however, and were quite reasonably afraid to return to Jackson County. As a result they were kept in protective custody in the Escambia County Jail in Pensacola at their own request. The reason they were still in custody was not widely known and when William Pickens of the NAACP passed through Marianna in early December of 1934, he was told by many black citizens that they were worried about what had become of the two women:

These women were abused by the mob, all their goods, except the poor rags on their backs, were destroyed, and then they were taken away to an unknown destination from the community at Marianna, many miles from Pensacola, so that the colored people of Marinna and Greenwood and that section were left whispering to each other trying to surmise the fate of these unfortunates. When Mr. Pickens passed through Marianna, colored women asked him in whispers: Do you know what they did to them two women, Have they done kilt them, too?" He did not learn until he arrived in Pensacola that they were in jail there, - really incommunicado.[8]

The account given by the reporter was somewhat inaccurate, as the two women were already in the Pensacola jail at the time their house was burned and they were never "abused by the mob" as Sheriffs Chambliss, Harrell and Gandy kept them away from the mob at all times. Otherwise, however, the report provides a fascinating insight to the worry about the two women among residents of Marianna's black community.

Pickens notified NAACP secretary Walter White of the concern voiced about Sallie and Annie Smith. The NAACP office in New York promptly wired Governor Dave Sholtz in Tallahassee to inquire about their status. The governor telegraphed a reply on December 6, 1934:

FIFTH STATES ATTORNEY JOHN H CARTER JR MARIANNA ADVICES ME THAT THERE ARE NO CHARGES AGAINST ANNIE SMITH AND SALLIE SMITH AND ACCORDINGLY THEY HAVE NO INTENTION OF BRINGING THEM BACK TO MARIANNA (STOP) HE ADVISES ALSO THAT TO AVOID ANY POSSIBLE DANGER THESE WOMEN ARE BEING HELD IN PENSACOLA TEMPORARILY WITH THEIR OWN CONSENT HAVING NO OTHER MEANS OF SUPPORT.[9]

Now possessed of reliable information on the status of the women, Pickens continued on to Pensacola where he secured a meeting with them:

When William Pickens reached Pensacola, he found that the mother and aunt of Claude Neal had been put into the Pensacola jail "for safe keeping." It was rather to shut their mouths, and prevent them from "telling." They were being held, so the sheriff said, "until things died down and became quiet." He admitted that there were no charges against these women. Yet they had been held for nearly a month, (Without a change of clothing.) All their goods and effects had been destroyed by the mob, which burned down their home and threatened them with murder – after nameless insults. All because these two women were relatives of the man whom the mob had already brutally lynched.[10]

The reporter this time engaged in quite a bit of hyperbole and stretching of the facts. The truth was that the two women were in Pensacola for their safety and could have left at any point they wished, but that they were afraid and had no way of living. They were, of course, originally arrested for far more serious reasons than simply being relatives of Claude Neal.

Primarily interested in providing a place for the women in better conditions than the county jail, Pickens called on the black community of Pensacola to open its hearts and hands to Sallie and Annie Smith:

William Pickens in a public address called for volunteers to form a committee to take care of these women, to take them out of felon's cells, out of the hands of Jailers, and to "relieve the sheriff of their expenses and care." He gave the first donation to start the fund.

The women of Pensacola rallied to the call, and preparations were being perfected to put the women into a local old folk's home, pending a time when they can get work and get again on their feet. Neal's mother is an old woman. The other relative is young.[11]

The reporter accidentally reversed the ages of the two women, but otherwise the account of the effort by Pensacola's black community is accurate. The two women left the jail, thanks to the efforts of William Pickens of the NAACP and the kind heartedness of the women of the black community in Pensacola. Many of those helping were poverty stricken themselves, but in the Christian way they sacrificed to help two women in worse need than they were themselves.

The tax books at the Jackson County Courthouse show that Sallie and "Katie" (one of Annie's nicknames) Smith continued to pay the property taxes on Sallie's land in Jackson County from 1934 until 1940, six years after the lynching. Beginning in 1941, the taxes were paid by Rilla Long, the daughter of Sallie Smith. The property that year was valued at $360.[12]

The truth, therefore, of what happened to Sallie Smith's 40-acre farm is that she continued to own it until 1941, when it was passed on to her daughter, Rilla Long. The latter woman was listed as Sallie's daughter on the 1900 census. By 1930, Rilla had married George Long and started a family of her own.[13]

The names of Rilla and George Long surfaced in an unexpected place in 1935. George Cannady, Lola's father, was arrested on charges that he fired a pistol at his niece, Dora King, from the front porch of the house. Rilla Long and another woman were walking along the road past the Cannady place when the incident took place:

...I don't know why he shot at me but he had been mad with us ever since it happened. He had a crazy spell in February or March and cursed us for everything and accused us of hiring the negro to kill his daughter and said he was going to kill us if he had to burn the house, that he had $350.00 to pay out with and the whole community heard it, I suppose fifty people heard that he said that. I don't know why, that was the first knowing he was mad with us about the murder that we know, and he cursed us, claimed my two brother-in-laws helped to do it and that papa hired the negroes to do it.[14]

Dora King's claim that her Uncle George blamed her father and two of her in-laws for Lola's murder electrified many in the media. Newspapers once again ran stories about the Claude Neal killing, now questioning whether an innocent man had been lynched in Jackson County.

The *Cleveland Plain Dealer*, for example, ran a piece that literally pointed out Dora's father as the murderer. "Now, after all that has happened and his slayers have gone unpunished," reported the paper, "new evidence comes to light that points to Lola Cannidy's uncle as her slayer." The article went on to claim that George Cannady "had sought legal permission to kill King and two other persons in Greenwood because he believed they had a part in killing his daughter, Lola."[15]

The actual trial transcript includes absolutely no reference at all to the claim of the Cleveland paper that George Cannady tried to get "legal permission" to kill Dora King's father. It does include a claim by Dora that at some point he offered to pay anyone who would do it for him.

People actually at the Cannady house when the alleged assault took place told a very different story of what happened than did Dora. Lola's mother said that her husband had started carrying a pistol after Lola was killed. He was about to go feed the hogs on April 19, 1935, when he looked at this pistol and commented that he had not tried it out since he had gotten

148

it back from the gunsmith in Bascom who was doing some repairs on it. According to Mrs. Cannady, he then went out on the porch and fired a couple of shots at a tree in the yard to test the weapon. Others at the house told similar versions of the event.[16]

George Cannady testified that he had never fired at Dora King or anyone else that day and that she had misinterpreted things:

...(W)hen I got ready to go feed my hogs I got up and got my corn out, and got the pistol and the cartridges was cankered and I told Simmie, "I believe I'll try the pistol and see if the cartridges will shoot," and shot twice at the root of the tree 15 steps from the porch, and another bullet went on kind of in the middle of the tree, and the bullet on the south glanced kind of southeast quarter of the tree, kind of glanced around in that way...[17]

Dora King and several other young women were then engaged in burning off an area of woods several hundred yards north of the Cannady house. This was a common practice in those days as it kept down underbrush, got rid of snakes and generally helped keep the woods clean for free-roaming livestock. The girls testified that they heard gunfire and Dora told the court that she could hear George Cannady swearing at her. She went on to say that several of the bullets hit in the dirt right around her. If true, this would have represented remarkable shooting by Cannady, since he was firing an old .38 caliber revolver with a 4 inch barrel from a distance of several hundred yards away. In fact, a private detective later found lead slugs in the tree in the yard, right where George Cannady said he had fired them.[18]

Cannady said on the witness stand that he had not been cursing at Dora King, who he was not even aware was in the vicinity:

...(T)hem negroes was coming down the road, two negro women, - Johnson and Rilla Long, and I cursed a word or two but didn't curse the negro women, just cursing at them, and told them to tell George and Everett Long to fix the fence or get out. I said, "You can't make a crop with the fence lying on the ground and the posts flat down," and down that way since Lola was killed and I says, "If you don't I am going to sue you and take that land away from you," and I went in the big gate and kept going south and in the woods pasture to feed my hogs."[19]

Several of the other witnesses reported seeing Johnson and Rilla Long in the road by the Cannady house at the time of the incident. Strangely neither the prosecution nor the defense in the case called them to testify. Cannady was convicted of assault and sentenced to several years in state prison. It was a tragic event in the life of all concerned, especially for a man who was prone to mental breakdowns from the time of his daughter's death until his own death years later.

The testimony from the case, however, provides several fascinating details about the murder of Lola Cannady, lynching of Claude Neal and the subsequent use of Sallie Smith's land in Jackson County. The statements of George Cannady and other witnesses clearly reveal that the land was being farmed by family members of Sallie Smith's just six months after the lynching. Rilla Long and her husband George were living on the land, as were Everett and Johnson Long. Cannady, in fact, was upset with them because the fence that bordered their land had been down since the time of the mob gathering at the farm and the Longs had not repaired it. Livestock was entering his fields and he was angry about it. The trial testimony provides solid evidence that Sallie Smith's own daughter and son-in-law were farming her land following the lynching and had not been driven from it, nor had the property been taken from them.

The statements by Dora King that George Cannady was angry with her family and had accused her father and two of her in-laws of "hiring the negroes" to kill Lola attracted media attention for an obvious reason. Reporters did not talk to him about the claim, however, or they would have learned that George Cannady suffered horribly from depression and what can only be described as temporary breakdowns following his daughter's death. At one point or another, family members say, he blamed pretty much everyone in Jackson County for having been involved in her murder. The real source of his anger with his in-laws in the King family, they say, was that he became convinced that they had been in contact with the Committee of Six. George Cannady believed that the men of the lynch group had "done him wrong" by not bringing Claude Neal to him still alive and he blamed the Kings for the decision.[20]

There is no physical evidence linking the King family to Lola's murder and none of Claude Neal's relatives has ever produced evidence that he was paid to commit the murder. Members of the King family, likewise, dispute the claim, saying only that Cannady "lost his mind after Lola was killed."[21]

As has been noted, the ownership of Sallie Smith's 40-acre farm passed to her daughter, Rilla Long, by 1941. She continued to pay taxes on the land until December 14, 1951, when she sold it to James F. King for $700.00, a fair market price for the time. The deed for the transfer of the property notes that Rilla Long was a widow by the time she sold the land. The deed further includes the notation that Mrs. Long "has good right to sell and convey the same; that it is free from lien or incumbrance in law or equity, and that the said party of the first part (i.e. Rilla Long) shall and will warrant, and by these presents forever defend the said lands unto the party of the second part (i.e. James F. King), his heirs and assigns against the lawful claims of all persons whomsoever."[22]

The tax records of Jackson County for 1934-1951 and deed transferring title of the land at fair market value show conclusively that Sallie Smith and her family did not lose their farm because of the violence surrounding the Claude Neal lynching. Mrs. Smith's daughter, Rilla, was farming the land with her husband and in-laws within six months of Neal's death and continued to do so for nearly twenty more years.

Sallie and Annie Smith did lose the value of the contents of the home they occupied in 1934 when it was burned by the mob. There is no way of knowing the value of the items lost, but if the family was typical of other poor rural families of the area, then the monetary worth of the personal property lost would not have been high.

News of the new FBI investigation of the Claude Neal lynching became public on October 22, 2011, when the *St. Petersburg Times* released a major article on the new inquiry. That same night a story detailing the new probe and providing information on the history of the 1934 incident, as well as the murder of Lola Cannady, also was released on the author's website, www.exploresouthernhistory.com. The news was picked up by newspapers and websites around the world, with the exception of those in Marianna. As of November 2011, neither of Marianna's newspapers had published stories about the new FBI investigation.

The *Tallahassee Democrat*, in a second round of coverage, published parts of an interview with Orlando Williams, Sr. Williams was quoted as saying that he and his family wanted $77,000,000 in compensation for the death of Claude Neal and the alleged loss of the family's farm following the lynching. According to the article, Williams arrived at his figure by multiplying the number of years that have passed since the lynching (77) by $1,000,000, an amount he believes is equitable as an annual value of the losses that he says were suffered by his family. To date, neither the Florida Legislature nor the U.S. Congress has introduced a bill authorizing such compensation.

As of the completion of this book in November of 2011, the FBI investigation of the Claude Neal lynching remained underway and no formal statement had been made regarding the expected date by which it would be concluded. Likewise, no formal information had been released on the anticipated results of the inquiry. Persons close to the investigation, however, indicated in off the record conversations that the probe was nearing its conclusion and that no arrests were expected. The inquiry, they said, would likely conclude that Neal was lynched by a small party of men, all of whom are now deceased, and that all witnesses with first-hand information on the lynching are also dead.[23]

If this is the case, then the FBI will close its investigation with results not unlike those of the roughly 100 other "cold cases" reviewed by the agency. A Justice Department spokesperson indicated in a November 2011 media briefing that "few, if any, prosecutions" would result from the inquiries authorized by the Emmett Till Unsolved Civil Rights Crime Act.

---

[1] *St. Petersburg Times*, October 23, 2011.
[2] *Socialist Call*, May 14, 1938, page 8, and numerous other newspapers, 1934-1940.
[3] *Cleveland Plain Dealer*, April 17, 1942, p. 2.
[4] The details of the FBI investigation of 2011 are based primarily on confidential interviews with several Jackson County officials and with documentation provided to them by the agency.
[5] Interviews with John P. McDaniel, 2011 and Sarah Bruce Harris, 1982.
[6] Email communication, Orlando Williams, Sr., to Dale Cox, March 19, 2010, #1.
[7] King Interview.
[8] *Negro Star*, December 7, 1934, p.1.

[9] Gov. David Sholtz to NAACP, New York, December 6, 1934, Manuscript Division, Library of Congress.

[10] *Negro Star*, December 7, 1934, p. 1.

[11] *Ibid.*

[12] Jackson County Tax Books for 1934 – 1949, Jackson County Courthouse.

[13] *Ibid.*, Federal Census for Jackson County, Florida, 1900 and 1930.

[14] Testimony of Dora King regarding alleged assault of April 19, 1935, given in court on May 21, 1935, Trial Transcript from records of the Florida Supreme Court.

[15] *Cleveland Plain Dealer,* June 14, 1935, p. 2.

[16] Testimony of Mrs. George Cannady regarding alleged assault of April 19, 1935, given in court on May 21, 1935, Trial Transcript.

[17] Testimony of George Cannady regarding alleged assault of April 19, 1935, Trial Transcript.

[18] Testimony of various witnesses, George Cannady Assault Trial, Trial Transcript.

[19] Testimony of George Cannady regarding alleged assault of April 19, 1935, Trial Transcript.

[20] Testimony of various witnesses, George Cannady Assault Trial; Interviews with members of the Cannady family.

[21] King Interview.

[22] Uniform Warranty Deed for NW ¼ of NW ¼, Section 21, Township 6 North, Range 9 West, Jackson County, Florida, December 14, 1951.

[23] *Ibid.*

Conclusions

This book was written to provide an accurate history of the murder of Lola Cannady, the lynching of Claude Neal, the murder of Deputy Dave Ham and the Marianna Riot of 1934. Previous publications on the topic have focused almost entirely on the lynching and riot, while the other two murders have received minimal attention. None of the events of those two weeks in Florida history, however, can be interpreted with any degree of accuracy unless they are considered as parts of a complete story. Lola Cannady, Claude Neal and Dave Ham were all the victims of brutal murders. None deserved the fates they suffered.

While dispute over his role in Lola's murder continues to this day, Claude Neal gave multiple confessions to the crime and not a single shred of evidence has ever been produced to show that any of his statements resulted from coercion. His lynching was a murder and never should have taken place. He should have received his day in court where his fate would have been determined by a jury and the competence of the two lawyers arguing the case, not by a Committee of Six in a Jackson County swamp. Neal may have been a murderer. His own words and a considerable amount of physical evidence suggested that he was, but he also was a victim. Claude Neal was killed, not tried. And his lynching to this day remains a dark cloud over good people who had nothing to do with what happened 77 years ago at Peri Landing.

Dave Ham likewise was a victim. He died in the line of duty, but his death also was a murder. When Buford Mears drew a .32 caliber pistol and shot Deputy Ham on Thursday evening, October 25, 1934, he murdered a brave law enforcement officer and a dedicated family man. Only in his 30s, Dave Ham left behind a wife and family that mourned his death for the rest of their lives. His name is engraved on a stone monument at the Jackson County Sheriff's Department and on a simple headstone at Pope Cemetery in Sneads, Florida. His memory should be forever cherished in Jackson County. He was a man who gave his life for his neighbors, family and friends.

Perhaps the greatest victim of the three, however, was Lola Cannady. She lived only to the age of 19 before she was brutally raped and murdered at a hog pen within sight of her family's simple country home. So far as is known, Lola never hurt a soul. She attended Bascom Baptist Church and was much loved by her family and neighbors. She never had the chance to marry. She never had children. She never left the sandy soil of northeastern Jackson County to see if, like so many other women of her era, she could have a career and learn what life was like in other places. Her grave is unmarked.

Did Claude Neal murder Lola Cannady? He said that he did and he said it more than once. Not just to law enforcement officers, but to fellow inmates at the Escambia County, Alabama, Jail. The sheriff there even tried to warn him against confessing so freely to the crime, fearing that word might somehow get out. Neal's response was that he would rather die at the hands of a mob than spend months waiting in fear of the electric chair.

The physical evidence also pointed to Neal as the probable killer. Footprints led from the scene to his home. The broken stem and loop of his pocket watch were found near Lola's body. His hands were cut and scratched. A torn and bloody piece of his shirt was found at the scene and later matched to a blood-stained shirt found at his home. A blood-stained hammer, thought to be the murder weapon, was found at the man's house. And finally, he left his home and family and spent the night in a corncrib before anyone even knew Lola was dead or began to consider him a suspect.

The actual decision of his innocence or guilt should have been made in a court of law by a jury of his peers. For that reason, I will simply say that he was the most likely suspect and that when the rumor, innuendo and fabrication is cleared away from the case, almost all that remains points in his direction. The crime, however, took place before DNA and even fingerprint evidence had become part of the arsenal used by law enforcement to fight crime. Claude Neal was never tried for the crime and under the laws of the United States, he was innocent until proven guilty. He will always remain, in the eyes of the law, a suspect, not a convicted criminal.

By lynching Claude Neal at Peri Landing, the men of the Committee of Six assumed authority over both the law and their fellow citizens. They believed Neal was guilty and feared that a trial would lead to what they viewed as a travesty of justice. The Scottsboro case was very much on their minds when they decided to end any possibility that the man would be placed on trial. They feared the justice system because they were unsure if a jury would be allowed to make the final decision on Neal's guilt or innocence. "What if Communist lawyers had become involved like they did up in Scottsboro?" one of the last surviving members of the group asked me. "They might still be trying and re-trying that case today" Lola Cannady, he felt, deserved better.

He and the other five, he said, made an offer to Sheriff Chambliss to allow a trial to be held, provided the officer agreed to surrender Neal up to them once the verdict was announced. But, as he recalled, "Flake said no." The six men agreed deep in the woods that there would be no repeat of Scottsboro in Jackson County. They never anticipated the riot or any of the other chaos that followed their killing of Claude Neal. When they dumped Neal's body in the dirt near the Cannady house, they thought everything was over. They were wrong.

W.F. "Flake" Chambliss would not serve another term as Sheriff of Jackson County. He was a tough lawman of the old school, but he had angered too many people by trying to stand up for the law. Retired Sheriff John P. McDaniel probably summed it up best when he once pointed at Chambliss' photograph on the wall of his office and told me, "That man lost his job for doing his job."

Chambliss tried to stop the lynching. He moved Neal from place to place in an effort to protect him and flatly refused all overtures from the men demanding the prisoner. He protected Neal's mother and great aunt as well, likely saving their lives. On the day after Claude Neal was killed, he and his deputies faced an angry mob in Marianna and Flake Chambliss was fully prepared to die if that's what it took to stop the rioters from lynching Bud Gammon.

He had already demonstrated courage of a rare sort two days earlier when he leaped over the seat of a moving car and wrested a pistol from the hands of Buford Mears even as the car careened off the highway and crashed into an embankment. He desperately tried to save the lives of both his deputy and a convicted bank robber in the wake of that escape attempt. Both would die, but Mears would live to stand trial for the shooting.

W.F. Chambliss did his duty in October of 1934, but found himself the subject of criticism from just about everyone. The press was merciless in its treatment of him, many newspapers going so far as to suggest that he was even an accessory to the lynching. Howard Kester perpetuated this falsehood when he concluded – based largely on rumor and innuendo – that Chambliss had not done enough to protect Neal from the mob. Kester, however, made no mention of the shootout that left two men mortally wounded on the very night that Claude Neal was taken from the jail in Brewton.

That shootout on Highway 90 one mile west of Cottondale had much more to do with the lynching of Claude Neal and Marianna riot than any writer researching the incidents has ever thought. There is something curious about a bank robber, with close connections to northeastern Jackson County, being slipped a pistol even as the raiding party of men from the county was on its way to Brewton to bring back Claude Neal. It could have been a coincidence, but if so it was one of the strangest in the history of Florida.

The men that robbed the Bank of Malone were acquaintances of at least some of the members of the Committee of Six. The two survivors of the group confirmed this in the early 1980s, but that is all they would say about the matter. Without evidence, any attempt on my part to link the timing of the two events would be mere speculation. I can only say that it was an curious coincidence that a bank robber pulled a pistol and opened fire on Sheriff Chambliss and one of his deputies just as the events leading up to the lynching of Claude Neal began to accelerate.

The escape attempt distracted and overwhelmed the sheriff and his handful of deputies at a critical moment. Events began to accelerate out of control when the first shot was fired in the sheriff's car that night and did not slow until the end of the Marianna riot two nights later.

Howard Kester would continue his crusade for social justice and support of Socialist principals for the rest of his life. He was an activist for his cause and an effective one. Even when socialism and communism faded from what favor they enjoyed in America, he remained true to the movement. He was one of the fathers of the modern social justice movement and likely would smile on the "Occupy Wall Street" protests of 2011.

He was not, however, a trained investigator. He was a Socialist Party activist and activists always have agendas. Kester's agenda was to secure, as the NAACP requested of him, all the "gruesome details." While his report on the Claude Neal lynching was superficial and relied primarily on gossip, it somehow became the most trusted source for the hundreds of writers that have touched on the topic. It provided the basis for much inaccurate reporting about Marianna and Jackson County and the events that took place there in 1934. On the other hand, *The Lynching of Claude Neal* proved to be a major weapon in the fight to bring the practice of lynching to an end in the United States.

So much that is false or inaccurate has been written about the murder of Lola Cannady, the lynching of Claude Neal and the riot in Marianna that it is unlikely that this or any other book will ever clear away all the inaccuracies. Perhaps people are happier with fiction than they are with the truth.

When news of this book was included in the *St. Petersburg Times* article on the new FBI investigation of the Claude Neal lynching, I found myself subjected to blistering criticism and hate mail from people who assumed the book would somehow justify a horrible lynching. They apparently came to this conclusion based on a single comment I had made about one of the purposes of the book being to provide a detailed account of the murder of Lola Cannady as well as of that of Claude Neal. This, it seems, was enough to convince some that the book should be soundly condemned before anyone had even read it. We live in strange times.

Other people, some of them close friends, questioned whether it wouldn't be better to let the "sleeping dogs" keep sleeping. I can only say to them that the only way to really put the dog of 1934 to rest is for the truth to be known. I have tried to do that and have told the story of the murders of Lola Cannady, Claude Neal and Dave Ham to the best of my ability. Perhaps someone far more talented than me will one day write a book that will do better justice to them all.

For some reason that I can't really explain, I have felt the presence of one or more of the victims with me as I wrote different parts of this book. Perhaps it was because I spent so much time walking in their footsteps and trying to see the world through their eyes. I remember the sadness I felt standing by Dave Ham's grave in Sneads and thinking that we should do more to perpetuate his memory. An almost physical illness overcame me one afternoon when I made my way into the swamp near old Peri Landing to the tree where Claude Neal was killed. There is something dark and horrible about that place. Elderly friends used to tell me that the lynching tree was haunted. Perhaps they were right.

The one presence that touched me most of all, though, was a mental image that came to me at times. It was of a frail candle slowly fading and then flickering out. I kept looking for some trace of its light in the darkness, but once it flickered out, it never came back.

Lola Cannady, may you rest in peace.

Appendix One

Report of Sheriff W.F. Chambliss

W.F. Chambliss
Sheriff Jackson County
Marianna, Florida
October 31, 1934.

Hon. David Sholtz,
Governor of Florida,
Tallahassee, Florida.

My Dear Governor:

RE: Lynching of Claud Neal.

Following is a report of the events leading up to the lynching of Claud Neal, in chronological order, as requested by you. I will gladly elaborate this, either verbally or in writing.

THURSDAY, OCTOBER 18th

Miss Lola Canaday left home about noon to go to a water pump about one-quarter of a mile south of her home in a field, and did not return.

Neal went into a field south of his home just after dinner, and came back two hours later, changed his clothes, and went away from home. He spent that night in Mr. John Daniel's crib, after obtaining permission to do so. He worked for Mr. Daniel.

Family and friends of Lola Canaday searched all night for her, without success.

FRIDAY, OCTOBER 19th

6:00 A.M: Sheriff notified of missing girl.

6:30 A.M: Body of girl found in woods about one-eighth of mile southeast of water pump, with head crushed.

6:45 A.M: Sheriff views body in woods; and finds piece of cloth near body, which was fitted into Neal's shirt that night.

8:30 A.M: Coroner's jury impanelled.

8:30 A.M: Neal arrested on suspicion by Deputy Coulliette and brought to Marianna. He was transferred immediately to Chipley where he remained about an hour, and was then transferred to Panama City. When arrested, his watch ring was out of his watch.

9:00 A.M: Watch ring found in woods near where body was found, and turned over to Sheriff that night.

9:30 A.M: Dr. Hodges makes examination of body for coroner's jury, and reports that she had been raped and murdered – that she was bruised and lascerated.

10:00 A.M: Sallie Smith, great aunt of Neal, arrested by Sheriff and placed in Chipley; and Neal's wet clothes were taken from her house. She and Neal live in the same house.

11:00 A.M: Tracks of two persons along North and South fence discovered. One looked like a man's track and the other looked like a woman's track. Reported to Sheriff at 1:00 P.M.

12:00 noon: Dr. MacKinnon makes examination of body at request of Sheriff and State Attorney, and reports no signs of rape appear, but that she had had intercourse – no bruises or lascerations.

3:00 P.M: Checked up on whereabouts of white man named Calvin Cross, who was under suspicion, and absolved him.

4:00 P.M: Lola Canaday buried at Bascom.

5:00 P.M: Kitten Smith, Neal's mother, arrested by Sheriff and placed in Chipley.

7:30 P.M: Deputy Hamm, at Cottondale, phones Sheriff that suspicious looking cars are passing through Cottondale going toward Chipley and Panama City. Sheriff phones Sheriff Hobbs at Panama City to move Neal to Pensacola or some other safe place because mob is on way to get him. Hobbs transports Neal by boat to Camp Walton and from there to Pensacola by car, and turns him over to Sheriff Gandy. Mobs storm Chipley and Panama City jails for Neal within thirty minutes after he is removed from Panama City.

9:00 P.M: Piece of cloth fitted into torn sleeve of Neal's shirt, and the ring is fitted into the watch.

SATURDAY, OCTOBER 20th

2:30 A.M: Crowd of about 50 men come to Sheriff's home and demand to know whereabouts of Neal, but information is refused.

10:00 A.M: Sallie and Kitten Smith questioned at length by Sheriff and State Attorney, at Chipley Jail.

11:00 A.M: Sheriff persuades mob to leave Chipley jail, but they threaten to come back.

4:30 A.M: Proposition to Sheriff that if he will cut down size of guard transporting Neal after conviction mob would probably let him be brought to trial, flatly refused.

SUNDAY, OCTOBER 21st

10:30 A.M: Chipley Sheriff phones Deputy Davis that mob had been there that morning demanding the two Smith women, and were coming back with torches to cut into jail.

11:30 A.M: Kitten Smith admits washing Neal's clothes after he came back to the house from field, and says there was blood on clothes.

11:30 A.M: Deputy Davis left Chipley with two women and delivered them to Pensacola jail.

Monday, October 22nd

9:00 A.M: Circuit Court convened, and order made to re-convene grand jury Wednesday A.M.

2:00 A.M: Pensacola Sheriff phones Sheriff that Neal has made complete confession and implicated a negro named Herbert Smith of Malone, and requested Sheriff to arrest Herbert Smith and bring him to Pensacola to confront Neal. Sheriff immediately made investigation and located Smith.

9:00 A.M: Coroner's jury completed its investigation, and found that Lola Canaday was murdered by Neal and the two women.

9:00 A.M: Trial of criminal docket of Circuit Court begins. Malone bank robbers brought over from Chipley for jury drawing. Special venire drawn for bank robbers' case on Wednesday, and special venire drawn for Godwin murder case on Thursday. Grand jury subpoenas issued for Wednesday.

9:00 – 10:00 A.M: Pensacola Sheriff requested by wire and by phone not to let Neal sign written confession implicating Herbert Smith until confronted by Smith and further investigation made here. Pensacola Sheriff advises he is sure Smith implicated, and requests that he be brought to Pensacola that night to confront Neal.

10:00 A.M: Deputy Coulliette requested to investigate whereabouts of Smith on day of murder, and, if circumstances suspicious, Sheriff would pick Smith up at dark and take him to Pensacola without knowledge of people.

11:00 – 2:00 P.M: Smith's movements day of murder found suspicious; whereupon he was taken into custody by Coulliette and brought to Marianna and immediately transferred to Tallahassee jail.

Neal makes written confession implicating Smith.

TUESDAY, OCTOBER 23rd

Criminal cases tried in Circuit Court all day. That night, Smith transferred from Tallahassee to Pensacola, through Georgia and Alabama, and turned over to Pensacola Sheriff to confront Neal.

WEDNESDAY, OCTOBER 24th

9:00 A.M: Grand Jury convenes, but recesses until Friday. State Attorney not prepared to submit case to them because of no word from Pensacola Sheriff concerning further implication of Herbert Smith.

10:00 A.M: Trial of three Malone bank robbers begins and continues all day.

Neal confronted by Smith, and admits that Smith had nothing to do with crime. Smith held in Pensacola.

THURSDAY, OCTOBER 25th

9:00 A.M: Trial of Malone bank robbers consumes most of day; jury convicts all three at 4:30 P.M.

5:00 P.M: Jury impanelled to try Godwin first degree murder case, and witnesses sworn.

7:00 P.M: While Sheriff and Deputy Ham are transporting two of bank robbers back to Chipley, Mears pulls pistol which was concealed on his person and shoots Deputy Ham, and Ham shoots McKinney, the other robber.

Neal amends written confession by leaving Herbert Smith out of it.

FRIDAY, OCTOBER 26th

8:00 A.M: Sheriff advised by phone by Pensacola Sheriff that mob stormed Bruton, Ala., jail at 2:00 A.M., got Neal, and headed toward Milton, Fla.

9:00 A.M: Trial of Godwin murder case held up on account of absence of Deputy Ham, a material witness for the State.

Ways and means of saving Neal from mob discussed and considered, but whereabouts and destination of mob not known.

SATURDAY, OCTOBER 27th

5:00 A.M: Bank robber McKinney dies at Marianna hospital of wounds.

6:00 A.M: Body of Neal discovered by Sheriff hanging to tree in Court House grounds. Taken down by Sheriff and taken to jail yard. Body was cold; had been dead some time. Now understand that dead body was hung there just before daylight.

8:00 A.M: Marianna full of people, demanding to see body and demanding that it be hung up again; all of which was refused by Sheriff. Circuit Judge requests that crowd be permitted to view body at the jail in orderly manner, which was done.

9:30 A.M: Circuit Court adjourned on account of mental condition of people, and the five criminal cases were continued until Tuesday, Oct. 30th.

10:00 A.M: Body of Neal buried.

12:00 noon: Negro named Bud Gammons seized by angry mob of about 100 white people at Court House, which accused him of striking a white man with a bottle. Deputy Sheriff Davis rescued Gammons from mob and got him into Sheriff's office on second floor of Court House. Mob storms office, demanding the negro be taken from the Sheriff and lynched. Sheriff manages to hold them off, with aid of several good citizens, Circuit Judge Lewis, Justice Buford of the Supreme Court, and others. About an hour required to quiet down this mob, and negro held in office.

12:00 – 3:00 P.M: Numerous outbreaks against negroes in Marianna, consisting of kicking them off the streets by crowds of white people, mostly drinking, and mostly from Alabama and Georgia, and surrounding counties. These mobs forced their way through several private dwellings searching for negroes, and presented themselves to numerous business establishments in Marianna demanding the negro employees. Several business men kept them out at the point of a gun.

12:30 P.M: Deputy Sheriff Ham dies in Chipley of wounds inflicted by Mears.

167

2:00 P.M: Lots of talk about lynching Mears for killing Deputy Ham. Mears (and Dudley) moved from Chipley to Panama City for safe-keeping; and brought back to Chipley about 9:00 P.M.

4:30 P.M: Troops arrive, and order restored.

6:00 P.M: Negro Gammons moved from Sheriff's office to Jail, guarded by troops.

SUNDAY, OCTOBER 28th

1:00 A.M: Mears and Dudley brought from Chipley jail to Marianna jail, under guard of troops.

Everything quiet; part of troops leave.

MONDAY, OCTOBER 29th

9:00 A.M: Malone bank robbers sentenced to life imprisonment; and taken back to Chipley jail, guarded by troops.

1:00 P.M: Negro Gammons released from jail, after ascertaining that he would be safe at home.

Remainder of troops leave at dark.

TUESDAY, OCTOBER 30th

9:00 A.M: Trial of criminal cases resumed in Circuit Court.

WEDNESDAY, OCTOBER 31st

After ascertaining that Herbert Smith would be safe at Malone, he was brought back from Pensacola and released.

The two negro women are yet in custody of Sheriff Gandy, of Pensacola.

I have not been able to learn any of the details of the Neal lynching; and do not know whether he was killed in Alabama or Florida. I am making further investigation along this line, and will advise you of results.

Yours very sincerely,
(s) W.F. Chambliss
Sheriff, Jackson County

Appendix Two

Grand Jury Report of November 9, 1934

Friday, November 9th,1934.

CIRCUIT COURT OF JACKSON COUNTY,

FLORIDA; FALL TERM 1934.

TO THE HONORABLE AMOS LEWIS, JUDGE OF THE COURT:

In pursuance of the order of the Court, we again convened, on Monday, Nov. 5th, 1934, and were in session the entire day investigating the matters which came before us. We then recessed until Wednesday, Nov. 7, 1934, and were in session that entire day. Being unable to complete our investigations on that day we recessed until today. We have now completed all of our work; except our investigation of the death of Claud Neal, and we find that we have gone as far with that investigation as we can at this time.

We have not been able to get much direct or positive evidence with reference to this matter; practically all of our evidence and information being in the nature of hearsay and rumors. However, we find that Miss Lola

Cannidy was brutally raped and murdered in this County on the 18th day of October, 1934, by Claud Neal, a negro, and that Claud Neal came to his death in this County on the 26th day of October, 1934, at the hands of a small group of persons unknown to us; after being forcibly removed from the jail at Brewton, Alabama, about 175 miles from here, by persons unknown to us.

We find that the Sheriff of our County did everything within his power under the circumstances to protect his prisoner, and we commend him for his action in performing his duty.

We do not think anything can be accomplished by remaining in session longer at this time, but we are ready and willing to continue our investigation of this matter at any time additional evidence of a convincing and substantial nature can be presented to us.

In view of the situation, we ask that we now be dismissed, subject to being recalled for further action.

Respectfully submitted, this Friday, November 9th, 1934.

Lansing D. Carkhuff
Foreman

W.A. Webster
Clerk

Appendix Three

Sen. Mary Landrieu's Comments on the Floor of the United States Senate regarding the Claude Neal Lynching

Sen. Landrieu's highly inaccurate account of the lynching was given on the floor of the U.S. Senate in support of the passage of a resolution offering an official apology by the Senate for its failure to pass anti-lynching legislation during the 1930s. It is given here as an example of the nation's perception of the crime.

June 13, 2005.

APOLOGIZING TO LYNCHING VICIMS AND THEIR DESCENDANTS.

...Forty-two years and thousands of lynchings later is the case of Claude Neal of Marianna, FL. After 10 hours of torture, Claude Neal "confessed" to the murder of a girl with whom he was allegedly having an affair. For his safety, he was transferred to an Alabama prison. A mob took him from there. They cut off his body parts. They sliced his side and stomach. People would randomly cut off a finger here, a toe there. From time to time, they would tie a noose around him, throw the rope over a tree limb. The mob would keep him there in that position until he almost died then lower him again to begin the torment all over.

After several hours, and I guess the crowd exhausted themselves, they just decided to kill him. His body was then dragged by car back to Marianna, and 7,000 people from 11 States were there to see his body in the courthouse of the town square. Pictures were taken and sold for 50 cents a piece.

One might ask, how do we know all the grizzly details of Claude Neal's death? It is very simple. The newspapers in Florida had given advance notice. They recorded it one horrible moment after another. One of the members of the lynch mob proudly relayed all the details that reporters had missed in person. Yet, even with the public notice, 7,000 people in attendance, and people bragging about the activity, Federal authorities were impotent to stop this murder. State authorities seemed to condone it, and the Senate of the United States refused to act.

Appendix Four

1934 Statement of Key Black Leaders in Marianna

This statement was released to Marianna's newspapers by a group of the city's key black leaders in the wake of the murder of Lola Cannady.

October 26, 1934

Slaying Brings Disapproval of Colored Citizens

To the Editor,
Jackson County Floridan:

Allow us to say through the columns of your widely-read paper, that we, the colored citizens of Jackson county, Florida, do here and now, stamp our disapproval upon the brutal murder of one of our white citizens last Thursday near Greenwood, Fla. The family have our deepest sympathy, and the law our unstinted support, in bringing the guilty to speedy justice.

We do not condone crime in any form. We believe in, and teach our Race to be law-abiding citizens. We trust that the brutal act supposed to have been committed by one of our Race will not break that friendly and mutual relationship that exists among the white and colored citizens of Jackson county; one of the best counties in the State. We have the utmost confidence in the best white citizens of the county, and trust you have the same in us. We will ever strive and teach our Race to never betray that trust. We pray that you will get the guilty brutes and protect the innocent.

Your humble citizens,
R.W. Whitehurst, E. Harley, M. Robinson, W.R. Robbins, H.H. Fagan, W.P. Preston, M.L. Clay, R.T. Gilmore.

Source: *Jackson County Floridan*, October 26, 1934, p. 4.

Appendix Five

Pathe Newsreel Coverage of the Marianna Riot

Pathe, an important news provider of the 1930s, had a film crew in Marianna by chance on October 27, 1934. The film makers were returning from the American Legion Convention in Miami and filmed scenes of the riot. A copy of the film, obtained by the author, includes random scenes of chaos in Marianna as well as film of National Guard soldiers setting up machine guns on courthouse square.

Newsreel Not To Show Pictures of Negro Lynching
Pathe News Representatives Will Visit City Soon to Make Pictures

Following receipt here of reports that Pathe News, of New York City, whose cameraman made numerous pictures here last Saturday, planned to release newsreels of the lynching of Claude Neal, negro, in the northern part of Jackson county, Mayor Jhon W. Burton wired them as follows:

Pathe News,
New York, N.Y.
It has been called to our attention that it is your intent to release pictures of the negro recently lynched in this County. The good citizens of Marianna join me in asking that you please refrain from making this release, or if

already released, please to effect withdrawal. While these pictures were taken in our City, yet the outrage occurred some 20 miles beyond our City limits, and instead of being made the recipient of adverse criticism for a condition that was entirely beyond the control of our officials, we rather feel that we have suffered an invasion, and do not believe that we should be made to suffer further the mal –advertising that will be occasioned by the release of these pictures. In the interest of justice, that a majority of good citizens may not suffer for the indiscretion of the minority, we ask that you please indulge us to the extent of not releasing these pictures.
JHON W. BURTON, Mayor.

Over long distance yesterday morning, Mr. C.R. Collins, of the Pathe News, in New York City, advised Mayor Jhon W. Burton that unfortunately release of news pictures had been effected before the arrival of Mr. Burton's telegram, but while they had pictures of the lynched negro they certainly would not allow them to be shown, and only such pictures as applied to regular news stories were being used. Mr. Collins assured mayor Burton that nothing had been released, nor would be released, that, in his opinion, would tend to bring an additional condemnation upon the good citizens of our City.

Mr. Collins also advised our Mayor that he had been authorized by his immediate superior, President Smith, to acquaint us with the fact that sometime in the near future he expected to send special representatives to Marianna to secure pictures and release a specially prepared story that will tend to give the entire world an altogether different viewpoint of our community than the one now prevalent.

Our entire citizenship should be most appreciative of the spirit of this good news agency in adopting this most friendly attitude towards us.

Source: *Jackson County Floridan*, November 2, 1934, p. 1.

Appendix Six

Lynching Reunites Sheriff with Brother

Perhaps the oddest result of the news coverage of the Claude Neal lynching was the reunion it made possible between Sheriff W.F. Chambliss and his brother.

Lynching of Negro Brings News of Brother Missing More than Generation.

Sheriff W.F. Chambliss Gets Letter from Relative Long Mourned as Dead

FORMER RESIDENT IS NOW IN CALIFORNIA

Jesse Chambliss Reads Story of Disorder Here and Writes Sheriff

Lifting the veil of silence that for more than a generation had kept unknown the whereabouts of a brother, long mourned as dead, the lynching of Claude Neal, negro, in Jackson county a fortnight ago has had a compensating influence upon the lives of at least three Florida persons. They are Sheriff W.F. Chambliss, of Marianna; J.R. Chambliss, of Tampa, and Mrs. Pattie Hartsfield, of Greenwood.

179

They have heard almost miraculously, from their brother, Jesse Chambliss, whom neither has seen in thirty-five years. The net result, according to gleeful anticipations in the hearts of the three Floridians, may be a reunion of the brothers and sister in this state in the not too far distant future. Jesse Chambliss, oldest of the four children, according to a communication received from him a day or so ago, is now located at Milton, Calaveras county, California.

The lynching of Neal, which gained front-page space in newspapers all over the country, caught the eye of Chambliss, he has written. The initials of the Jackson County sheriff were the same as that of the brother, whom Jesse Chambliss knew in the days of his youth and early manhood. Consequently, he wrote to Sheriff Chambliss a few days ago, asking details of the affair, and wanting to know whether the official had suffered any physical harm in attending to his duties. Further, he sought details as to the other brother and sister, asked about the associates and friends of his youth and made inquiry concerning the old family home in Alabama.

Coming like a voice from the tomb, the communication for the nonce completely perplexed Sheriff Chambliss, so he at once got in touch with the sister at Greenwood. After alternately rejoicing and weeping over the communication from the long-lost brother, they did not wait for the slow processes of mail delivery to communicate with the one whom they had long regarded as dead. They telegraphed him at Milton, telling him that the children were all alive and well, and asking for further information concerning the activities of the one who drifted away from this section so many years ago. They now await this information, which is soon expected....

Source: *Jackson County Floridan*, November 16, 1934, p. 1.

Photographs

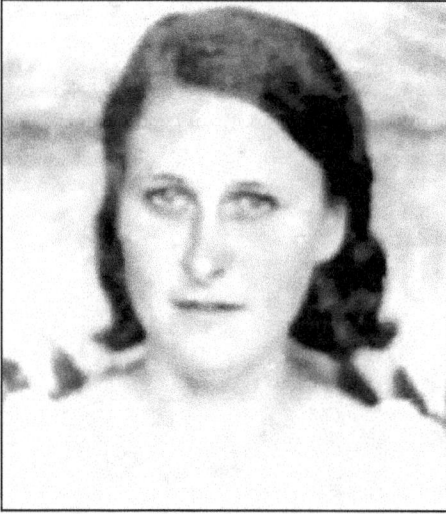

Lola Cannady
Thought to have been taken the year before her death, this faded photograph shows the young woman as she likely appeared at the time of her murder in 1934.

Cannady Family
This photo, taken after Lola's murder, shows Bessie, Raleigh and George Cannady. Notice the "dogtrot" style of the house, with the open central hallway.

Murder Site in 1988
This was the location of the hog pen where Lola Cannady was attacked and killed on October 18, 1934.

The Hog Pen Pump, 1988
Lola was working at the pump when she was approached by Claude Neal. It was a hand pump in 1934, but was later replaced by the electric one seen here.

The Discovery of Lola's Body
This photo of Bessie Cannady was taken when her daughter's body was found on the morning of October 18, 1934. The logs cover the body.

The Wood Lot.
The scene where Lola's body was found was wooded in 1934, but is now a plowed field.

185

Cannady House, 1988
*The house, since demolished, was a focal point of events following
Lola's disappearance and murder.*

Cannady House Site, 2011
*The site of the house is now a plowed field, seen here planted with cotton in
2011. The same crops are grown on the farm today as in 1934.*

186

Bascom Baptist Cemetery, 2011
Lola Cannady was buried here on the day her body was discovered.
Her grave is unmarked.

Smith House Site, 2011
The home of Sallie Smith stood here in 1934.
It was burned to the ground on the night that Claude Neal was lynched.

Jackson County, 1932

This map shows Jackson County as it appeared in 1934 when the murders
took place. The Cannady farm was just north of Greenwood.

AF&G Railroad at Malone

The line of the AF&G can be seen in the map at the top of the page.
The railroad connected Greenwood and Malone with Dothan, Alabama.

Lynching Tree at Peri Landing
*Claude Neal was tortured and killed at this oak tree in the Chattahoochee
River swamps near today's Parramore Landing Park.*

Aerial View of the Lynching Site
Peri Landing was located on the river bend shown here. The lynching site was in the woods at the upper left of the photograph.

Bare Spot at the Lynching Tree
A commonly told legend in the Parramore area holds that nothing will grow on any spot where Claude Neal's blood was spilled.

190

Dozier Road in Jackson County
*The car carrying Neal's body to the Cannady farm after the lynching
followed this route. He was placed on the back bumper for the trip to the
farm from Peri.*

Cannady House, 1988
*Sheriff John P. McDaniel (at left) examines the spot where Claude Neal's
body was left. He studied the murders for historical purposes prior to his
retirement.*

Old Jackson County Courthouse
This was the courthouse in use in 1934, but no longer stands.
The tree from which Claude Neal's body was hanged can be seen at left.

Marianna from the Air, 1930s
The riot took place in the streets around the courthouse, seen near
the center of the photo. The jail is visible at the bottom center.

**Justice Rivers Buford
Florida Supreme Court**
*Justice Buford saved lives during the
Marianna riot by bravely standing
down the mob at the doors of the
Jackson County Courthouse.*

Scene of Buford's Stand
*Justice Buford stood down the mob at the front doors of the courthouse,
through which deputies had just taken Bud Gammon after rescuing him
from the mob. Rioters were about to use a battering ram on the doors.*

Dave Ham
Sheriff's Deputy
*Deputy Ham died in
Chipley on the day
of the Marianna
riots and was buried
the next day.*

Deputy Ham's Grave in Sneads
*The deputy's simple grave is at Pope Cemetery in Sneads. His wounding in
the attempted escape of the Malone bank robbers added confusion and
chaos to the situation in Jackson County.*

Historic Image of Downtown Marianna

This photograph shows Confederate Park as it appeared in the 1930s. The clerk at the Chipola Hotels saw beatings taking place here.

Chipola Hotel, 2011

The hotel was one of the finest in Florida in 1934. The park visible in the photograph at the top of the page can be seen at left.

Amos Lewis
Circuit Judge
Judge Lewis presided over the grand jury that investigated the murders of Lola Cannady, Claude Neal and Dave Ham.

Dave Sholtz
Governor of Florida
A friend and ally of President Roosevelt, Sholtz ordered the National Guard to Marianna

Primary References

Articles

Jones, Walter C., "Obama Administration Stands Up to Lynching Challenge," Online Athens, July 22, 2011.

Documents

Brantley, Dan, Statement given to Hugh M. McCaffey, Governor B.M. Miller Papers, Alabama Department of Archives and History (Transcription from E.W. Carswell Collection).

Byrne, G.S., Statement given to Hugh M. McCaffey, Governor B.M. Miller Papers, Alabama Department of Archives and History (Transcription from E.W. Carswell Collection).

Cannady, Bessie (Mrs. George), Testimony in the Circuit Court for the Fourteenth Judicial Circuit, May 21, 1935, Florida Supreme Court (George Cannady Appeal).

Cannady, George, Testimony in the Circuit Court for the Fourteenth Judicial Circuit, May 21, 1935, Florida Supreme Court (George Cannady Appeal).

Carson, J.M. and E.P. Sanchez to William Pickens, November 5, 1934, Papers of the NAACP, Part 7, Series A, Reel 9.

Carter, John, Manuscript Notes, Slade West Collection.

Chambliss, W.F., Report on the Lynching of Claude Neal, October 31, 1934, Author's Collection.

Confession of Claude Neals, October 22, 1934, Governor B.M. Miller
Papers, Alabama Department of Archives and History (Copy
from E.W. Carswell Collection).

Governor's Office Phone Log for October 1934, Florida State Archives.

Jackson County Grand Jury, Docket Book 3, Jackson County Archives.

Jackson County Grand Jury, Presentment, November 9, 1934, Jackson
County Archives.

Jackson County Tax Books, 1934-1949, Jackson County Archives.

Jeter, Lum, Statement given to Hugh M. McCaffey, Governor B.M. Miller
Papers, Alabama Department of Archives and History
(Transcription from E.W. Carswell Collection).

Kester, Howard, to Walter White, November 7, 1934 and November 13,
1934, NAACP Papers, Part 7, Series A, Reel 9.

King, Bessie, Testimony in the Circuit Court for the Fourteenth Judicial
Circuit, May 21, 1935, Florida Supreme Court (George
Cannady Appeal).

King, Dora, Testimony in the Circuit Court for the Fourteenth Judicial
Circuit, May 21, 1935, Florida Supreme Court (George
Cannady Appeal).

Landrieu, Sen. Mary, Speech on the Floor of the U.S. Senate, June 13,
2005, *Congressional Record.*

Shanholtzer, Jake, Statement given to Hugh M. Caffey, Governor B.M.
Miller Papers, Alabama Department of Archives and History
(Transcription from E.W. Carswell Collection).

Sholtz, Gov. Dave, Telegram to NAACP, December 6, 1934, Manuscript
Division, Library of Congress.

Stanley, Cara Bell, Testimony in the Circuit Court for the Fourteenth
Judicial Circuit, May 21, 1935, Florida Supreme Court
(George Cannady Appeal).

State of Florida vs. Hubert Mears, Harrison McKinney and M.F. Dudley,
Trial Records, Jackson County Archives.

State of Florida vs. Rudolph Godwin, Grand Jury Indictment, Fall Term,
1934.

State of Florida vs. Rudolph Godwin, Motion for Mistrial, October 26,
1934.

Strong, R.A., Statement given to Hugh M. Caffey, Governor B.M. Miller
Papers, Alabama Department of Archives and History
(Transcription from E.W. Carswell Collection).

U.S. Censuses for Jackson County, Florida, 1900 and 1930.

Uniform Warranty Deed, Rilla Long to James King, Jackson County, Florida, December 14, 1951, Jackson County Archives.

White, Walter, to Howard Kester, October 31, 1934, NAACP Papers, Part 7, Series A, Reel 9.

White, Walter, to Gov. B.M. Miller, November 22, 1934, NAACP Papers, Part 7, Series A, Reel 9.

Interviews

Bascom Area Resident, October 28, 2008 (Name withheld by request).

Beall, Roy, Sr., December 12, 1984.

Cannady Family Member, December 23, 1995 (Name withheld by request).

Committee of Six Member, #1 (Name withheld by request).

Committee of Six Member #2 (Name withheld by request).

Cousin of Claude Neal, July 16, 1990 (Name withheld by request).

Cousin of Lola Cannady, July 16, 1990 (Name withheld by request).

Cousin of Lola Cannady, November 28, 1999 (Name withheld by request).

Crime Scene Eyewitness, October 15, 1990 (Name withheld by request).

Family Member of Phil Coulliette, July 28, 1984.

Friend of Lola Cannady, August 15, 2011 (Name withheld by request).

Harris, Sarah Bruce, 1982.

Jackson County officials, Current and Former, 2011 (Confidential Sources)

Jackson County Residents, 1982-1990 (Names withheld by request).

Kester, Howard, July 22, 1974, Interview B-0007-1, Southern Oral History Program Collection (#4007), UNC-Chapel Hill.

King, James, October 28, 1990.

McDaniel, John P., 2011

Neighbor of Cannady Family, 1986 (Name withheld by request).

Parramore Area Residents, 1982-1986 (Names withheld by request).

Winslett, John, September 12, 1934.

Newspapers

Augusta Chronicle, October 22, 1934.

Cleveland Plain Dealer, June 14, 1935; April 17, 1942.

Dallas Morning News, October 28, 1934.

Dothan Eagle, October 26, 1934; November 1, 1934.

Free Lance-Star, October 27, 1934.

Jackson County Floridan, October 19, 1934; October 26, 1934; November 2, 1934; November 9, 1934.

Marianna Times-Courier, October 27, 1934.

Miami News, August 22, 1934.

Negro Star, December 7, 1934.

New Orleans *Times-Picayune*, October 28, 1934.

Panama City Pilot, October 25, 1934; November 1, 1934.

St. Petersburg Times, October 23, 1934; October 28, 1934; November 2, 1934.

Sarasota Herald-Tribune, November 1, 1934.

Seattle Daily Times, October 21, 1934; October 26, 1934; October 28, 1934.

Socialist Call, May 13, 1938.

Sunday Oregonian, October 28, 1934.

Tallahassee Democrat, November 1, 1934.

The New York Times, August 26, 1934; October 28, 1934.

Personal Communications

Orlando Williams, Sr., to Dale Cox, March 19, 2010, #1.
Orlando Williams, Sr. to Dale Cox, March 19, 2010, #2.
Orlando Williams, Sr. to Dale Cox, March 19, 2010, #3.
Orlando Williams, Sr. to Dale Cox, March 23, 2010.

Publications

Barnes, Jeffrey G., "History," *The Fingerprint Sourcebook*, U.S. Department of Justice.

Cox, Dale, *Old Parramore: The History of a Florida Ghost Town*, Bascom, 2010.

Federal Writer's Project of the Works Projects Administration for the State of Florida, *Florida: A Guide to the Southernmost State*, Oxford University Press, 1939.

Furie, Mik, "The Ballad of Claude Neal," The Dark Furie Blog, February 10, 2010.

Kester, Howard, *The Lynching of Claude Neal*, New York, 1934.

McGovern, James W., *Anatomy of a Lynching*, Baton Rouge, 1982.

Books by Dale Cox

Available in Print & Kindle editions.

The Battle of Marianna, Florida
A detailed history of the 1864 Civil War battle that culminated the deepest penetration of Florida by Union troops during the entire war.

The Battle of Natural Bridge, Florida
A history of the battle that saved Tallahassee from capture and preserved its status as the only Southern capital city east of the Mississippi not taken by Union forces during the Civil War.

The Battle of Massard Prairie, Arkansas
An account of the 1864 Confederate attacks on Fort Smith, Arkansas, this is the only book-length treatment of these little known actions that opened the door for the greatest supply seizure of the Civil War.

Old Parramore: The History of a Florida Ghost Town
A look back through time at the fascinating rise, life and disappearance of a riverboat town on the forgotten Florida section of the famed Chattahoochee River.

Two Egg, Florida: A Collection of Ghost Stories, Legends & Unusual Facts
The stories behind the stories of some of Northwest Florida's must unique legends, including the true history of the quaint little community of Two Egg.

The Early History of Gadsden County
A fascinating look at a series of key episodes from the pre-1865 history of Gadsden County, Florida.

The History of Jackson County, Florida: The Early Years
(Volume One)
A look at the pre-Civil War history of Jackson County, focusing on Spanish missions, Native American history, the Seminole Wars, the Antebellum era and more.

*The History of Jackson County, Florida: The Civil War Years**
(Volume Two)
The most detailed account ever written of a Florida county's experience during the four years of the Civil War. Details battles, raids, outlaw gangs and more.

*Also subtitled *The War Between the States*.

A Christmas in Two Egg, Florida
A short novel or redemption set in the quaint Northwest Florida community of Two Egg.

All books by Dale Cox are available at:

www.exploresouthernhistory.com

Index

124, 125, 126, 128, 131,
132, 133, 136, 142, 145,
148, 149, 155, 156, 157,
159, 160
Raleigh, 7
Wilford, 9, 11, 37
Carson
J.M., 133
Carter
John, 24, 26, 32, 35, 43, 49,
63, 94, 108, 113, 119, 123,
142, 145, 146
John, Sr., 114
Cartledge
L.H., 105
Casey
James, 143
Cawthon
A.A., 105
Chamber of Commerce, 68
Chambliss, 119
W.F., 17, 18, 19, 23, 25, 26,
31, 32, 33, 34, 35, 36, 37,
41, 43, 47, **48, 49**, 63, 65,
79, 86, 87, 88, 89, 94, 96,
97, 104, 105, 108, 111, 112,
113, 114, 117, 118, 122,
123, 136, 141, 142, 145,
146, 157, 158
Chattahoochee, 62
Chattahoochee River, 62, 84, 104
Chevrolet Caravan, 66, 98
Chicago, 36, 66
Chipley, 19, 23, 25, 27, 32, 33,
34, 48, 49, 50, 54, 63, 97, 106,
136, 145
Chipola Hotel, 67, 98, 122, 123
Chipola River, 104
Civil War, 122
Claude Neal, 142
Cleveland Plain Dealer, 148
Columbus, 62

Committee of Six, 62, 64, 72, 74,
75, 77, 78, 80, 81, 84, 85, 114,
116, 118, 127, 128, 135, 142,
150, 155, 157, 158
Coombs
J.P., 108
Percy, 119, 132
Cooper
J.C., 87, 92, 96, 105
Cottondale, 27, 28, 37, 48, 63,
87, 97, 158
Coulliette
Phil, 18, 19, 20, 23, 35, 37,
123, 132, 142
County
Bay, 26, 29, 97
Calhoun, 95
Escambia, 29, 34, 35
Escambia (Alabama), 9
Escambia, Alabama, 37
Gulf, 29
Jackson, 1, 2, 4, 5, 6, 7, 17, 18,
19, 20, 25, 26, 28, 31, 33,
35, 41, 43, 44, 45, 47, 53,
54, 61, 63, 65, 72, 92, 99,
100, 103, 105, 111, 112,
113, 116, 119, 128, 131,
136, 141, 143, 145, 150,
151, 155, 156, 158, *See*
Washington, 19, 28, 32, 123
Cowarts, 5
Cox
Van, 117
Criggers
T.J., 55
Croker sacks, 5
Cross
Calvin, 25, 112
Cummings
Homer S., 104
Dallas Morning News, 104
Daniel
John, 39, 112